THE INTERVALS OF ROBERT FROST

THE INTERVALS OF ROBERT FROST

A Critical Bibliography by
LOUIS AND ESTHER MERTINS

With an Introduction by
FULMER MOOD

UNIVERSITY OF CALIFORNIA PRESS
Berkeley and Los Angeles
1947

UNIVERSITY OF CALIFORNIA PRESS
BERKELEY AND LOS ANGELES
CALIFORNIA

◇

CAMBRIDGE UNIVERSITY PRESS
LONDON, ENGLAND

COPYRIGHT, 1947, BY
THE REGENTS OF THE UNIVERSITY OF CALIFORNIA

All Rights Reserved

No part of this book may be reproduced in any form
without permission in writing from the publisher

Contents

ROBERT FROST AND THE MERTINS COLLECTION, *by Fulmer Mood* 1

INTERVALS, *by Louis Mertins*
   San Francisco Interval 5
   Lawrence Interval 13
   Derry Interval 18
   Dymock Interval 24
   Amherst Interval 29
   Cambridge Interval 34
   Hanover Interval 36

BIBLIOGRAPHY, *by Esther Mertins*
   Poems 39
      Lawrence Interval 39
      Derry Interval 39
      Dymock Interval 40
      Amherst Interval 43
      Cambridge Interval 54
      Hanover Interval 57
   Marginalia 59
   Books 61

INDEX 85

Robert Frost and the Mertins Collection

THE COLLECTOR and the author whose works have been collected joined hands to build the Mertins collection. The first piece of Robert Frost's work that Louis Mertins acquired was the manuscript of "Stopping by Woods on a Snowy Evening." He had this by gift from the poet in 1932. Frost had just returned to California for his first visit since 1885, when his mother had taken him, a ten-year-old boy, from San Francisco to Lawrence, Massachusetts, where their Frost kin were living. In the summer and fall of 1932 Robert Frost was at Monrovia, California, and there Mertins made his acquaintance soon after the poet's arrival from New England. The two men were often together, and they became fast friends. In November, Frost left Monrovia for Amherst, Massachusetts. At Christmas, 1932, he surprised Mertins with an inscribed copy of the *Collected Poems* (1930). After these initial gifts, he did not forget his friend in California, but made still other gifts, including first editions and manuscripts. Thus the foundation of the collection was well and truly laid, with Frost's assistance at the beginning. Almost annually thereafter, at Christmas time, the poet sent Mertins something for the collection, now a book, now a manuscript poem. And nearly every December there came also a Christmas booklet containing new verses by Robert Frost. Thus by degrees the superstructure of the Mertins collection was fashioned. As it grew, the poet maintained his interest in it and never failed (with but one understandable exception) to send Mertins a copy of the first edition of every book his publishers brought out.

In August, 1941, Louis and Esther Mertins paid a visit to New England. They called first at the farm near Derry, New Hampshire, where Frost had composed much of his early poetry. There they photographed the birch tree of which the poet has written in "Tree at My Window." They took other photographs, too, including one of the stone wall celebrated in "Something there is that doesn't love a wall." The poet afterward obligingly identified all the pictures with appropriate notes. By so doing he kept up a gracious custom of some years' standing; since 1932 he had been in the habit of annotating his gifts to his friend. Most of the items, indeed, carry his autographic comments. These glosses have high value for biographical and critical purposes.

From Derry the travelers drove to Frost's Vermont farm near Ripton, where the poet welcomed them and in the course of an evening's conversation found opportunity to inquire after the progress of the collection. By chance that night he uttered a remark which pointed the way toward its augmentation in the future. Would it not be desirable, he asked, to collect the issues of the several periodicals in which his poems had first appeared?

This was a project that appealed to Mertins, who set to work to realize it on his return to California. He had dealers' shops to visit, dealers' lists and catalogues to scan. Before

INTRODUCTION 3

many months passed, Mertins acquired an impressive number of periodicals, both English and American, every one of which contained a poem by Robert Frost. There was keen pleasure to be had in the gathering of these dusty periodicals, but Mertins was best pleased when he received a copy of the New York *Independent* for November 8, 1894, the number which carries "My Butterfly: An Elegy." The poem is Frost's earliest to appear in a magazine of national importance.

By degrees Mertins sent these magazines to Frost, who was already familiar with some of them. Others he saw for the first time. The handling of these issues brought about an upwelling of Frost's literary memories, and in turn he annotated each with a relevant comment or an inscription which cast light on the poem thus treated. These jottings by the poet further enhance the literary value of the Mertins collection. Many of them are reproduced in the bibliographic section of this book.

Today, the collection is kept at the owner's ranch house, which stands on the northern slope of Smiley Heights overlooking California's San Bernardino Valley. From the library windows on the second story an amazing sunlit panorama opens out before the eye—rows of orange trees in the foreground, the broad sweep of the valley's floor in the middle distance, and beyond, the massive brown bulwark of rocky crags beneath the brilliant sky. Here, for the time being, the collection remains. But its owner intends, eventually, to transfer it to the University of California. At Berkeley it will come to rest with other library treasures within sight of hilly San Francisco, the natal city of Robert Frost.

FULMER MOOD

Neither Out Far nor In Deep.
The people along the sand
All turn and look one way;
They turn their back on the land;
They look at the sea all day.

Some say the land is more,
But whatever the truth may be,
The water comes ashore
And the people look at the sea

They cannot look out far;
They cannot look in deep;
But when was that a bar
To any watch they keep.?
                Robert Frost

THE POET'S HANDWRITING

An early manuscript version of
"Neither Out Far nor In Deep"

The Intervals of Robert Frost

SAN FRANCISCO INTERVAL
1875–1885

THE EDITOR of a California newspaper once said to me, "You know, the mystery of Robert Frost is this: though born a Californian, he has been able to get it completely out of his system. The voice that speaks through him is no longer the voice of the State where he was born, but the voice of New England."

Has Frost succeeded in getting California out of his system? Are there not echoes in his poetry of that brief interval when a small boy roamed the San Francisco hills, and gazed away toward Lone Mountain and Tamalpais, or played around the chimpanzee cages at Woodward's Gardens, or watched the breakers rolling in on the sand at Land's End?

Few persons think of R. F. as a California poet. And it must be admitted that, when all his verse is taken into account, New England is in it a good deal more than his native state. Born in San Francisco in 1875, he became a New Englander ten years later. Nevertheless there are poems that stem from a happy childhood in San Francisco, when the poet was

> One of the children told
> Some of the dust was really gold.

If the boy Robert Frost wrote any verse before he left California at the age of ten, it has happily been suppressed. Certainly it was never printed. His first printed poem, published in the Lawrence (Massachusetts) High School *Bulletin,* was pure fancy, with no earthly habitat. At his graduation from high school in 1892 the class hymn, signed by him, was published, and was sung (with music by Beethoven) at the exercises. This is patently a New England product, as his use of the word "runnel" shows.

But there are a few poems which the poet has admitted as Californian, and others which he suggests were written at the time of his only visit to California between 1885 and 1947—that is, in the Olympic year, 1932. For example, there is that fine poem, "Neither Out Far nor In Deep," first published in the *Yale Review.* He later used it for one of his Christmas cards. Most of it was written in California—to quote his own words, "when we were round together"; and he gave me the early draft of the MS, now one of my most precious treasures. The printed poem showed certain alterations which we shall note.

Critics have written of the magical changes wrought by Frost in three of his poems. In one of these, "Nothing Gold Can Stay," the changes were mutations that are at once discernible when one places an early draft MS (comparable to the MS we are considering) beside the poem as it appeared in a magazine. In the other two, "Into Mine Own" (entitled in the book, "Into My Own") and "November Guest," the changes were made between their first appearance in magazines and their inclusion in Frost's first book. The alterations were of words, or sometimes of entire lines, or were no more than exchanges of plural for singular forms of nouns.

To me, at least, the changes between first draft and printed form of "Neither Out Far nor In Deep" show as great loss as gain. One stanza is added which to me seems out of place. Moreover, the smoothness of the whole is not helped by the adding of one word to a line, though it must be admitted that what is lost in smoothness is gained in strength:

> When was that ever a bar

is much more forceful than the original

> When was that a bar.

Other changes are noteworthy. The semicolons of the original draft become periods. In the first line of the second stanza (third stanza in the printed form) we read,

> Some say the land is more.

This is altered to

> The land may vary more.

In line 2, "whatever" becomes "wherever."

Although Californian, this is a composite poem. According to the author, it grew out of an afternoon we spent together, happily remembered by the poet when inscribing *Contemporary American Men Poets,* published in 1937. He wrote: "R. F. to L. M. to remind him of the day we went down the coast [of California] together." But it is not altogether the outgrowth of that day. It was first printed in the *Yale Review,* and in the copy of that magazine in my collection Frost has written: "This was one of my few Californian poems. But it is made of mixed memories. Take care of the MS of it I gave you, Louis. R. F." When the poem appeared in the magazine, editorial liberties were taken with it. The original was printed without change in the *Citizen* (now perhaps one of the rarest of rare Frostana); on my copy the poet has written, "Pleasure to make this over to you a second time, Louis. Robert Frost, New England, 1944."

Another poem which genetically is Californian (so admitted by its author) is "Once by the Pacific," which first appeared in the *New Republic*. He has written in my copy of the magazine almost the same words he wrote by the other poem in the *Yale Review*, "One of my few Californian." However, the first grew out of later, the second out of earlier, memories. "Once by the Pacific" came from remembering a terror occasioned by the swelling ocean that threatened, at the Cliff House, to engulf shore and destroy continent. This sea fear lingered with him through the years.

Frost's astounding memory always startled me. I turn to my diary for September 8, 1932, and go over the account of his reading to me at his Monrovia home, at the Greystone house, his new poems on which he had lately been engaged. The entry says: "Then he started reading, and for an hour I heard these new poems, some of them humorous with that sly Frost humor, some infinitely sad, some of incident, some of characterization, and the most of them about scenes and snow and mountains, and moon and stars. One of the sun shining down through a cloud with the snow as lacework back and forth was especially lovely."

Two years later this last-mentioned poem appeared in the

SAN FRANCISCO INTERVAL

Yale Review under the title, "After-Flakes." Just why he remembered, unless association of ideas suggested to him our evening together, I do not understand. But (in 1946) he has placed it genetically in California by writing in my copy of the magazine in which the three poems, including this one, appeared: "L. M. I believe I wrote the third of these in California when we were round together." The third was the poem with which we are dealing.

Again, on the same date, I find an entry in the diary: "He asked me which I liked best of them all, and I said I believed the one about the two shoes, one wet with the waters of the Atlantic at the end of Long Island, the other at Cliff House San Francisco." This poem, "A Record Stride," appeared in the *Atlantic Monthly* for May, 1936. Again he remembered and over against the line "In a Vermont bedroom" he has written the amplifying words "South Shaftsbury," while opposite the line "The other I wet at the Cliff House" (he underscored Cliff House) he has set down, "or Long Beach rather." He made this notation in 1944. He had visited me in Long Beach in 1932.

There are two other poems on which he had at least been working when on this first visit to California. One was "The Bearer of Evil Tidings." I recall that this (always one of my favorites) was in a rather unfinished state, as was also "The Literate Farmer and the Planet Venus." These stem, therefore, from his native soil. "Just to think," he has written in my copy of the *Atlantic* in which the "Literate Farmer" appears, "just to think of it! I had read this to Louis Mertins ten years before I ever sent it to be printed." When I came upon the original of this poem in the collection of a friend, the very page he had read to me, I unblushingly broke the Tenth Commandment.

It does appear, therefore, that California memories and experiences have made good their claim on Robert Frost as a poet. The voice may be the voice of New England, but the hands (often the heart) are Californian.

I fail to find any indisputable echo of California in Frost's first book, though I have long toyed with the idea that seeds were sown in the mind of the ten-year-old boy on that April day in 1885 when his father died—seeds of his Swedenborgian mother's scattering. I have not given this up, despite the poet's written denial that he had his father in mind when he composed "Trial by Existence." That denial ("No, I didn't have any relative in mind") was penned by him on my copy of the old *Independent* containing the poem. All of *A Boy's Will* is redolent of New England. Perhaps he was not old enough to go back to earlier memories. These came much later.

There is even less chance of finding a memory of his San Francisco childhood in *North of Boston*. Here New Hampshire is speaking. We recognize persons, places, incidents, characterizations. But these, also, came out of a later Interval—the Derry,—which he has termed "our brook interval."

We would scarcely expect a California memory in *Mountain Interval*. There may be an echo of the Dymock Interval in "The Sound of the Trees"—critics long have maintained that the sound was that of the Ryton firs in the West Midlands. I cannot fully agree. But there is no sound of the waves

SAN FRANCISCO INTERVAL

at Land's End in this book; no sight of the fogs lifting above the Golden Gate. These poems speak of the Plymouth days, "beyond the Covered Bridge."

By the same sign *New Hampshire* is ruled out. None of the dust that falls here "is really gold." Of them all, only the poem "To E. T."—admittedly of the Dymock Interval—is away from New Hampshire.

But when we reach *West-running Brook* we begin to find echoes of the poet's birthplace. They come first in "A Peck of Gold":

> Dust always blowing about the town
> Except when sea-fog laid it down,
> And I was one of the children told
> Some of the blowing dust was gold.

Again (and I have mentioned this already) we meet an echo of California in "Once by the Pacific," where we are moved by the lines

> You could not tell, and yet it looked as if
> The shore was lucky in being backed by cliff,
> The cliff in being backed by continent;
> It looked as if a night of dark intent
> Was coming, and not only a night, an age.
> Someone had better be prepared for rage.
> There would be more than ocean water broken
> Before God's last *Put out the Light* was spoken.

To hear the poet read this is to understand the overwhelming terror which in the heart of a small San Francisco boy gave birth to the poem in memory long afterward.

Could it be that "Bereft," with its magical

> Looking down hill to a frothy shore

echoed the death of his father? There *must* be echoes in "Sand Dunes," though "fisher town" sounds like the Maine coast.

Definitely when he made the collection for *West-running Brook* California had entered his poetry. But there was more to come.

Upon the publication of *A Further Range* he was thinking of California, even when he wrote the dedication to "E. F.," for he said there, "Beyond the White mountains were the Green; beyond both were the Rockies, the Sierras..." And it is accentuated in his inscription of the first edition which he sent me almost the day it left the press: "For Louis Mertins, as a surprise, this, my secretly published (as distinguished from privately printed) book about California among other places. Ever his Robert Frost." Here we come upon that which is San Franciscan in flavor as well as title—"At Woodward's Gardens"; for, with his little sister, he often visited there on sunny days. Our poet is turning back to a golden childhood.

There is little to write of *A Witness Tree,* except to admit that only in the poem "The Literate Farmer and the Planet Venus" do we have a California echo.

More and more as he approaches his diamond jubilee Frost in memory turns back to the city of his birth. On the flyleaf of an ancient volume of mine, a book of sermons by the Rev. John Doughty, his childhood pastor (he could never remember whether he was baptized once or twice in the Society of the New Jerusalem), he has written his still-green memories of his Leavenworth Street home, the pastor's house, and (after sixty-two years) a complete description of that "good man." He even remembered the location of his own house (with Doughty's a block away), counting the houses from the corner.

Once he nearly returned to live in California. But that was long ago, and is another story.

LAWRENCE INTERVAL
1885–1900

THAT CHILL November day in 1894 which saw the *Independent* arriving from New York at the Frost home, 96 Tremont Street, in Lawrence, Massachusetts, marked the advent of a new and notable name in American letters. Seeds planted in California, bulbs set out in New England, were beginning to come to flower. The poetic urge of genius (and painstaking craftsmanship) had started on its way to market.

Robert Frost never, until the Modern Library editors discarded it, gave up his first published poem. Others of this and the Derry Interval he eventually disclaimed, sought to obliterate: to "My Butterfly: An Elegy" he clung to the last. It formed one of that small group of poems which he gathered into a tiny fardel, privately printed, called *Twilight* (only one copy of which has come down to us); it was included in *A Boy's Will,* later in *Collected Poems*. Once he recorded that some of the lines of this early eclogue he liked as well as any he had ever done.

In my copy of the *Independent* for November 8, 1894,

where "My Butterfly: An Elegy" occupies the coveted first column left, page 1, I find he has written, as if in confirmation of that which he had said previously: "To Louis Mertins. Kay Morrison found it for you. These were the lines that set me on my way. That's why I kept the poem in my first book. R. F." He has never said why he retained it in succeeding collections. Perhaps it was for the same reason.

These were laggard weeks for the poet in the Lawrence Interval—days of dreaming—the gift of idle hours. A boy develops with his surroundings in such periods; in such years bents are established. It was so here.

This Interval presents to us the only time our poet "rushed into print." But youth, whose thoughts are long, long thoughts, has so little time. Only age is unhurried. One grows old so quickly at fifteen, things change so rapidly.

Roaming up and down the Merrimack, he was absorbing the landscape in all seasons, learning flowers, trees, and birds, not out of books, but by observing and remembering. Such knowledge has always remained the astonishment of his friends.

Aside from inconsequential verses, some of them published in the high school *Bulletin,* Frost wrote a few of measurable value, including "Caesar's Transport Ships" and "Warning," which were published later in the *Independent*. These he failed to preserve for us.

With no outward sign from the poet, with only certain inward evidences to guide us, we find a few poems scattered over a long period of publication which would appear to be rooted in the Lawrence Interval. Of these, among his

LAWRENCE INTERVAL 15

earlier ones, the style's the thing. The subject matter could be of any location. The style is definitely in progress. To mention a few: "Stars," "Ghost House," "Love and a Question," "Hannibal," "The Flower Boat."

There is less certainty when we come to "Pan With Us." But the aura of the classics is still plainly about him here. For that matter, so it was when, long afterward, he finished "Build Soil," plainly a page under the Hellenic aegis. But of one thing we need express no doubt: some of the lines were patently altered after the Lawrence Interval. "The whimper of hawks beside the sun" is far from juvenile. A line like that doesn't just happen. However, the inception of the poem is one with "Caesar's Transport Ships" and others of the Interval. Of this we feel reasonably sure.

The Lawrence graveyard, where lie the bodies of Frost's grandfather and grandmother, his father, his mother, and his sister Jeanie, holds the citadel position of the factory town. When all the low-lying city is swathed in a cloud of smoke from the belching of innumerable chimneys, the cemetery hill is looking on the sun. That the poet had the Lawrence burying ground in mind when he wrote the "Disused Graveyard" seems possible, though this likewise was made up of "mixed memories."

We are on much more familiar ground, genetically, when we reach *A Lone Striker*. This was Lawrence, and the youth who was bobbin watch and night watchman in these same factories was at last remembering them. On the blank last page of my copy (No. 8 of the Borzoi Chap Books published by Alfred Knopf) the poet wrote an early draft of "Neither

Out Far nor In Deep" quite a while before he projected it in print. (See the plate following page 3.) He also wrote a table of contents in his own hand. The roots of this poem are deep in the Lawrence of his boyhood. How many lone strikers he must have known!

There is one poem which for obvious reasons we want to treat more fully. We find much internal, and not a little external, evidence for placing in the Lawrence Interval the genesis of "The Quest of the Orchis," published in the Derry. He speaks of skirting "the margin alders for miles and miles." Certainly the swamps around Lawrence more nearly fit this expression than does the Derry scene. Moreover, since the poem was published as early as 1901, it would have been much too soon for it to have been inspired, written, redacted, and brought to print within the Derry Interval. On the published copy of "A Moth Found in Winter" (which in the collection he has dated "1900") he has scribbled, "You can't get me to believe this happened in Derry." In my copy of the *Independent* containing "The Quest of the Orchis" he wrote: "I had almost forgotten this when I came on it a few years back and put it into one of my later books. This R. L. Frost sounds like a stranger to me. Doesn't he to you, Louis?" This poem was signed "R. L. Frost," a perhaps unique style.

The book he referred to as having included this poem was not the brochure *Three Poems* (in which it had its first separate printing), but *A Witness Tree,* in which it was entitled "The Quest of the Purple-Fringed." Between its first appearance in the magazine in 1901 and its eventual inclusion in the book in 1942, significant changes were made. To begin with, in the second line "o'erhead" has become "overhead," in consonance with his almost universal shunning of the elision in later years. Or take the first and second lines of the third stanza. In the magazine we find

> Yet further I went before the scythes should come
> For the grass was high ...

In the book this is altered to

> Yet further I went to be before the scythe
> For the grass was high ...

In the first and second lines of the fourth stanza Frost, continuing in the path of the fox, originally wrote,

> Then at last, and following that I found
> In the very hour ...

But far more facile and smooth, after the change, are the lines as found in the book:

> Then at last and following him I found
> In the very hour ...

You see, he was really following the fox all the time, but it took him forty-one years to remember.

In the last line of the last stanza but one he has conjured up two added words to transform a dim line into a clear and bell-like one. In the magazine:

> Counted them all to the buds in the copse's depth
> Pale as a ghost ...

In the book:

> Counted them all to the buds in the copse's depth
> That were pale as a ghost ..

The poet was not pale as a ghost. It was of the buds he spoke.

In the first line of the last stanza, by changing a state of being into a manner of acting he has achieved smoothness, finish, beauty. It only needed the substitution of "silently" for "silent":

> Then I arose and silently wandered home.

Furthermore, and finally, he added to the strength of the poem by doing away with all line indentations.

Students of Frost seem not to have noted the kinship between this early poem and the lovely "Tuft of Flowers" which won him his place as a teacher at Pinkerton Academy, Derry. The two came out of the same thought, and internally are of the closest kin.

DERRY INTERVAL
1900–1912

I FANCY there is no combination of place and time in American literary history out of which has come so much pure poetry from one man as came out of Frost's years at the Derry farm. That pile of stones which called forth "Mending Wall" is as real as Bunker Hill Monument.

It is a lovely landscape, that which surrounds the West-running Brook. Those who admire the poet solely for his lines can only admire halfway. They must know the terrain out of which the poems were evolved—every curving valley, every little insinuating creek, every hump of the White Mountains stretching away into Vermont. For out of these grew the poems without which our American literature would indeed be Laodicean in its poverty. How portionless we would be did we not claim as our own "A Tuft of Flowers," "The Pasture," "Blue Ribbon at Amesbury," "A Linestorm Song," "Into My Own," "My November Guest," "Birches."

These poems are as much a part of the Derry Interval as Frost is a part of New Hampshire. How he took the "run-out mountain farm" as a gift from his grandfather, determined to give himself twenty years to become a poet; how he eked out a miserably insufficient existence on the short-thirty sterile acres of the old place two miles south of Derry Village; and how, almost to the day, a score of years saw him one of the outstanding poets of two continents—these things go into the making of a tale that is told.

But writing verse and publishing it were two different things. I find in my copy of the *Forum* for November, 1912, where "My November Guest" appears, that Frost has written, "Dear Louis: You say this was the twelfth poem I sold to a magazine. I suppose you have counted them. I take your word for it. R."

It wasn't that he didn't try. All those lean years on the farm, he was writing and mailing out poetry that has since taken its rightful place in world literature. But the sanctums which were open to innumerable nobodies were closed against a solitary *somebody* in literature. Twelve poems in eighteen years is a small showing. But when with a sudden swoop fame came upon him, his prophecy was fulfilled.

> They would not find me changed from him they knew—
> Only more sure of all I thought was true.

Whatever farm poems Frost may have written were delved out of the Derry earth. For here he was a farmer—"a real, though not a very good farmer," he once said. On all his other farms, agriculture was pure dilettantism. Poetry was first—poetry, and lecturing in this college and that. At Derry the poems were sweated out between farm work and farm chores. And whether he wrote them with a Franconia, a South Shaftsbury, or a Ripton background, even the later ones were written with an inner eye for the Derry scene.

Little of the poetry appearing in *A Boy's Will*, aside from that which had its origin in the Lawrence Interval, came elsewhere than from Derry. Reading these poems is like scanning a page from the autobiography of a "one-horse, one-cow farmer."

"Late Walk" is an integral part of Derry, as is "A Prayer in Spring," the two separated only by six months of winter. In "Flower-Gathering" we see Elinor White waiting for the truant feet of one who has been absent "for the ages of a day" as clearly as though he had called her by name. "Rose Pogonias," according to Derry legend (neither admitted nor denied by the poet), grew out of an afternoon tramp into the woods with a named fellow Derryite. "Mowing," "Going for Water," and "A Tuft of Flowers" have the seal of the Derry place upon them—pressed into the soft clay.

I cannot read "Storm Fear" and "Wind and Window Flower" without closing my eyes to get the picture of the Derry farmhouse interior—all safe abed,

> Those of us not asleep subdued to mark
> How the cold creeps as the fire dies at length.

DERRY INTERVAL 21

I can see the vast snowy world outside—"the comforting barn" adjoining the house at the southeast corner, with everywhere the woods closing down; and in the window the flower which Elinor has so carefully nurtured in its pot leaning aside and thinking of naught to say to the breeze which tomorrow will be "a hundred miles away."

In a different manner, for the matter also is different, *North of Boston* is almost, if not quite, wholly a Derry product. The poet seems occasionally to have demurred; as, for example, in my copy of the *Century Magazine* for July, 1916, containing "In the Home Stretch," he has written of the drawings by Adams, "The places resemble neither the Derry nor the Franconia farm in any least detail." This, it may be, is not a complete denial, or even a partial one, of the poem itself as being of Derry. But in the end he would be the last to deny that the poems "To the Thawing Wind," "Now Close the Window," "Home Burial," "Blueberries," "After Apple-Picking," "The Code," and "The Woodpile" are of this period. And Baptiste, in "The Axe-Helve," was a near neighbor and friend of the poet-farmer—just across the stone wall.

Running in a straight line eastward down the slope, up the hill past the orchard, the stone wall of the Derry farm *is,* together with the poem written about it, the Derry farm. Come spring, the poet, calling to his French-Canadian neighbor on the north, would go forth to repair the damage done by that "something that doesn't love a wall." "To each the boulders that have fallen to each." Nor did the two set the stones in place half so securely as the poet has placed these lines in the abiding letters of mankind.

Of later poems which indubitably stem out of Derry we should mention "Blue Ribbon at Amesbury," first printed in the *Atlantic Monthy* for April, 1936. In the copy of this magazine in the collection the poet has written: "You ask was this in Derry. How can you ask, Louis? R. F."

In *A Witness Tree* was printed "Trespass," which requires no imagination to place it at Derry—no more than to place "Tree at My Window" at the east window of the old house, even if we did not have the poet's identification of it on the picture.

Seldom were the drab days at Derry enlivened by the appearance of a check for a poem. Acceptances, however, did occasionally come. And while we are more concerned with the poems germinated in the Derry soil, we have an interest as well in those which flowered in the interval.

On June 27, 1901, the *Independent* came out with "The Quest of the Orchis," a poem we have already discussed at some length. Five heartbreaking years were to pass before the same magazine used "Trial by Existence," October 11, 1906. In 1907, Frost submitted a poem to the local newspaper, the *Derry News*,—a thing he seldom did. "The Lost Faith" was printed March 1, 1907. In October, one of the loveliest lyrics ever written came out in the *New England Magazine*—"A Line-storm Song." In its issue of March 26, 1908, the *Independent* made room for "Across the Atlantic." Frost came to regret having submitted this poem, and would have it die at last by "the slow smokeless burning of decay." "A negligible accident" is his summing-up on the page containing it in my copy of the magazine.

DERRY INTERVAL

In 1909 two periodicals opened their pages to him. How fortunate the editor of the *New England Magazine* in having that matchless poem, "Into Mine Own," placed in his hands! It was printed in May, 1909. I do not agree with those who think it a callow poem of undeveloped adolescence. It has more than craftsmanship in it. When he wrote it, Frost surely had the Derry scene before him in his inner if not his outer eye. To the west and south stood

> Those dark trees
> So old and firm they scarcely show the breeze.

Into their vastness he was determined some day to steal away, fearless of ever finding open land, or highway where the slow wheel pours the sand. But, alas for all his fancy, those dark trees *were* the merest mask of gloom; just a little beyond, though unseen from his vantage, lay another farm, open land and a farmhouse. But he was seeking to "run to hiding new." Of this poem he once wrote to me, drawing attention to it in his "very first book," and suggesting that here was the beginning of his desire to hide from something.

The other poem mentioned in this connection was "The Flower Boat," in the *Youth's Companion* for May 20, 1909.

There is another poem, published long afterward, which we do not have to conjecture about. I refer to "The Bonfire." Even if we did not have the poet's own holographic evidence, there is proof within the poem itself to place it in the Derry Interval. The children anxious for a little excitement, the father full of bravery "with the best of them"—these things are redolent of Derry. But the poet himself has spoken. In my copy of *The Seven Arts* for November, 1916, he has testified: "Yes, Derry was where I got the scare about a grassfire. I've had a worse one since in Ripton." So, Derry it was.

During the Plymouth period (which was not really an Interval, but only an interval between Intervals), preparations went on for publishing "October" and "My November Guest." But by the time the former came out on October 3, 1912, in the *Youth's Companion,* and the latter the following month in the *Forum,* the poet and his family were far away from it all, hiding in England.

DYMOCK INTERVAL
1912–1915

WHEN A SNUG company of poets gathered in the West Midlands of Gloucestershire in the summer of 1914, they little suspected that they were about to write a new chapter in Anglo-American literature. Lascelles Abercrombie was the titular head of the Georgian school of poetry. The group also included Wilfrid Gibson, Rupert Brooke, and John Drinkwater. All but the last joined the group at the triangle which had Dymock for a center. Frost was there at Gibson's insistence, living at "Little Iddens" farm, adjoining Ledington. Later, Edward Thomas came.

Brook Farm had no echo here, or Old Harmony. These men were individualists, not communists. Nor was there much of the spirit of the Lake Country and Windemere and Grassmere in the meetings of the clans. Plain living, high thinking, talk on noble themes, marked the gatherings in

DYMOCK INTERVAL 25

the Old Nailshop ("the Golden Room," as one of them named it memorably) at The Greenway.

It remained for Wilfrid Gibson to sketch for us his comrades-in-lines, so that we know them as they were. He published the poem, "The Golden Room," in the *Atlantic Monthly* for February, 1926. On the MS of this poem by Gibson (in the collection) Frost has written: "We must admit this was terribly nice of Wilfrid. He and I were neighbors away down in the country in 1913–14. I wonder how you found this copy of his poem all done out in his hand."

Before the summer was over the American poet had wellnigh become the dominant force. Abercrombie might offer "a quick flash"; Thomas could come forth with "a murmured, dry half-heard aside"; Brooke well may have contributed a "clear laughing word"; but always it was Robert Frost who went

> on and on and on
> In his slow New England fashion for our delight,
> Holding us with shrewd turns and racy quips,
> And the rare twinkle of his grave blue eyes....
> Again Frost's rich and ripe philosophy
> That had the body and tang of good draught-cider
> And poured as clear a stream.

The product of Frost's poetry during the Dymock Interval just about matched the produce of the "Little Iddens" farm. It wasn't much. "Here I wrote some poems," he has put it; but not all of them are traceable.

There was, of course, the unmistakable "To E. T.," printed in the *Yale Review* for April, 1920. In my copy of the magazine he has scribbled, "The second stanza comes back oftenest." When he wrote those lines, Edward Thomas, the poet-soldier, had already "met the shell's embrace of fire at Vimy Ridge." Before his friend died, however, Frost wrote for him that most-loved poem, "The Road Not Taken," which he sent in manuscript to E. T. in France.

Another poem with roots deep in the rich Gloucestershire earth is "Thatch." This more nearly comes intact out of the West Midlands than anything else Frost has given us. But "Iris by Night," first printed in the *Virginia Quarterly Review* (spring, 1936), is clearly of the terrain. Nor need we remain long undecided over what friend was with him when

> One misty evening, one another's guide,
> We two were groping down a Malvern side
> The last wet fields, and dripping hedges home.

The Dymock Interval, however, is more important to us for publication than for production. For within it, though none of the poems were written at the time, his first two books found a press.

How he decided, one winter night in 1912 as he sat before the fire in his Beaconsfield home (his poems spread out on the floor in front of him), that he would "run up to London and find a publisher," is an oft-repeated tale. As the result of an interesting experience too long to relate here, he decided to allow David Nutt and Company to publish him. It all seems so simple. But when we recall that Frost was an utter stranger from a faraway continent (the Georgians and the West Midlands, F. S. Flint, and Ezra Pound, and Harold Munro all were still in the future), the marvel that he succeeded grows on one.

That little volume, *A Boy's Will*, which David Nutt and Company brought out early in 1913, is one of the precious items of our literary heritage. A copy of the volume lay in Frost's trunk for nearly thirty years. Then he put his hand on it, still in mint condition, and sent me the inscribed copy for the collection.

David Nutt made but one printing of *A Boy's Will*, and a year later one printing of *North of Boston*. Their different issues (see the Bibliography, below) in later years, when the sheets were gathered and differently bound, form a study for bibliopoles. On the title page of *North of Boston*, in the collection, Frost has written above his signature the legend, "First Printing." On the half title of this copy he has written seven lines from "The Woodpile," ending with that beautiful expression,

> With the slow smokeless burning of decay.

In the Dymock Interval, several of Frost's poems appeared in Harold Munro's magazine, *Poetry and Drama*. Of these there is a story worth repeating. The editor arranged for "Readings of Poetry" in the Poetry Bookshop, Bloomsbury, where poets gathered to spend a literary evening. Admission was obtained by presenting a ticket, which was to be found laid in the magazine. One of these tickets, visaed by R. F., is in the collection. Passing the shop one evening, that first autumn in England, Frost saw that readings were booked. He decided to use his ticket and see how English poets did things. He stayed over, sat on the stairs, and met F. S. Flint. Flint wrote a letter to Ezra Pound, then in London, telling him about his fellow American. Pound in turn wrote to Frost, inviting him to come see him. Frost, always dilatory, put it off an unconscionable time. When he finally decided to see Ezra, it fell on the day the proof sheets of *A Boy's Will* were ready. The two went to the printers and brought them back. Pound read them through twice. Then he excused his visitor and wrote a review which he sent to *Poetry: A Magazine of Verse*—the first review of Frost ever printed in his native land.

As a direct result of Frost's attending the salon on this fateful night, in *Poetry and Drama* for December, 1913, Munro used "A Hundred Collars" and "The Fear." It would seem that Louis Untermeyer had his first knowledge of R. F. by reading this number of the magazine. A year later, Munro used a group of Frost's finest poems: "The Smile," "Putting in the Seed," "The Cow in Apple Time," and "The Sound of Trees." This was certainly giving the visiting poet a good send-off in a fine place to show poems. Undeniably, it in no wise hurt the sale of the books.

There is an interesting footnote here. In my copy of the *Atlantic Monthly* for August, 1915, Frost's first summer back home, the poet has written over against the group of poems ("Birches," "The Road Not Taken," and "The Sound of Trees"): "I think this was the first publication of all these poems. I should have been in trouble before this if it wasn't." But, regardless of his innocence in the matter, *Poetry and Drama* published "The Sound of Trees" exactly eight months before it appeared in the *Atlantic Monthly*.

When Frost returned to his own country, his harvest of

poems written in England was a slight one. But he carried with him something else gained from his companionship with the members of the Dymock group, something he had received so easily that he may never have known when it came to him. Those men established him with himself. Forever after, he could be sure of all he thought was true.

AMHERST INTERVAL
1916–1936

As we come to this period of Robert Frost's creative work we are on less firm ground than we were in the others. Proofs that this poem or that came out of the period are less easy to adduce.

I think the reasons for the uncertainty are well founded. One that stands out from the others is the poet's growth in complexity. The Frost who went to Amherst at the invitation of Alexander Meiklejohn in 1916 was a far more complex character than the Frost who "lived under thatch" in England, just as the boy who lived at Lawrence, and the youthful farmer-poet who tilled the soil at Derry, was simpler than the naïve individual who took his little poems to David Nutt.

Amherst was kind and generous to its professor of English—and continued so for two decades. He had leisure for writing, and here, besides no little verse, he wrote, and saw produced at near-by Northampton, his charming play, "A Way Out."

Uncertain though we are about the dates of composition of so many of the poems Frost wrote between 1916 and 1936, of some we may be sure. There is the poem "On the Heart's Beginning to Cloud the Mind." In my copy of *Scribner's Magazine* for April, 1934, the poet has scrawled, "I wrote this in a hotel in Wilkesbarre, Pennsylvania." To all intents and purposes this places the poem within those years.

I have intimate knowledge of the genesis of some now quite famous poems. These were printed in *Poetry: A Magazine of Verse* under the title "Ten Mills," in April, 1936. I was with the poet in 1932 when these were being written. He later sent me the early draft of one of them. "You had this in MS before it was printed," he wrote on the page containing this poem in my copy of the magazine. The poem (later published under the title "Untried," and again as "Waspish") is set down in the early MS merely as "Name Unnamed."

"The Lesson for To-day," published in *A Witness Tree*, was unquestionably inspired, if not written (both, it may be), in Florida on one of the poet's winter trips. On March 3, 1935, he wrote me a playful letter from Key West in which he described how he went out into the graveyard to view the stones. "The oldest person I could find," he wrote, "in the Key West graveyard yesterday (Sunday) was a veteran of the War of 1812 who died in Key West at 108 years. But many have lived to be older than that. His inscription wound up, 'A good citizen for 65 years.' He must have been a bad citizen for 43 years then. That's what undermined him and shortened his life.... I merely mean that in fifty years from now we'll be about at the end of our old age pensions."

AMHERST INTERVAL

Turning to the poem, we can see by comparing it with the letter that the idea was germinating in March, 1935, in Key West:

> It sent me to the graves the other day...
> But I was only there to read the stones,
> To see what on the whole they had to say
> About how long a man may think to live,
> Which is becoming my concern of late....
> One man had lived one hundred years and eight.

Frost in 1935 was beginning to ponder about longevity.

It must have been about this same date (which would have corresponded in historical time) that he wrote "A Serious Step Lightly Taken":

> It is turning three hundred years
> On our cisatlantic shore...

The first Frost landed in 1634.

However much or little he may have written in the Amherst Interval, certainly that extended period saw more publication than before: *Mountain Interval* (most of which went in manuscript with him to England in 1912); *New Hampshire,* and *West-running Brook.* It is interesting to note the rise of the curve of magazine publication as time for bringing out a new book approached.

Take the period just prior to the publication of his fourth book in 1923. All these published poems from 1920 to 1923 were included in *New Hampshire.* In 1920, ten were published in magazines; in 1921, fifteen. In 1922 there was an unaccountable drop to a single poem, but in the next year the number rose to eleven.

Now it is reasonable that, however long the period between creation and publication may have been, some of these were written in the period of publication. But in all, the roots by now were complex and interwoven. Some of the poems went back very far for a beginning, eventually to be completed under far different circumstances.

Just as he bombarded the magazine editors before the publication of *New Hampshire,* so he did again in the years which went before the appearance of *West-running Brook.* We cannot fail to observe that, the moment *New Hampshire* was out, the magazines had a rest. In 1924 he printed only one poem; in 1925, three. The number rose in 1926 to five; in 1927 it nearly doubled; in 1928 it dropped again to six. All these were included in *West-running Brook* when it came out in 1928.

It is at this point that we come upon an unexplained hiatus. The magazines entered upon a near-Sabbatical. Not a single poem of Frost's is to be found in any of them from 1928 to 1934.

Only once since his first poem was printed in 1894 had there been so long a period of silence. That was from 1901 to 1906. But this was a sterile six years as against the other record of five. Could the reason have been discouragement occasioned by the reviewers' neglect of *West-running Brook?* All we can do is accept the six years of nonpublication as a fact. These were troubled years for the poet, as I know from being with him at the time. Serious illness in the family, a changing administration at Amherst—these were factors that may have entered into his silence.

AMHERST INTERVAL 33

But as we have seen, nonpublication did not mean nonproduction. When in California, or at South Shaftsbury, or in Amherst, the poet was writing, revising, redacting.

There were mountain peaks of publication in the long Amherst Interval. In 1917 war was on. Frost was thinking a great deal about Edward Thomas, dead in France, and Rupert Brooke, dead in Greece. In January of that year the *Yale Review* published "Not to Keep." In the copy of this magazine in the collection the poet has written, "This and the Bonfire were my most ostensible war poems." In September following, the *Atlantic Monthly* published a notable poem, "The Axe-Helve."

Frost was really pleased when in 1920 (July and December) *Harper's Magazine* used eight of his poems. From what he wrote on my copy of the December issue it would appear that Joseph Anthony came in person for the poems and did not wait for an uncertain, or at best a laggard, submission.

What joy it is to come upon old favorites in ancient magazines—favorites like "Hillside Thaw," "Witch of Coos," "Paul's Wife," "Stopping by Woods on a Snowy Evening." Even the poet seems to have shared this feeling of elation. On my copy of the *New Republic* for March 7, 1923, where the last-named poem appears over his signature, I find him exclaiming, "Why, why! I had forgotten this." Again, on my copy of the same magazine for January 12, 1927, where "A Winter Eden" appears, he has written, "Interesting to meet these old ones again."

In 1936 the long Amherst Interval was to come to an end. The "bridge pier in the middle of the river" was about to be removed. The magazines again were giving space to his poems, which betokened the publication of a new book. And in this year Harvard University appointed him to the Charles Eliot Norton professorship of poetry.

CAMBRIDGE INTERVAL
1936–1943

WHEN FROST went to Cambridge, the Harvard man was but coming home. He had gone to Dartmouth as a boy out of high school because his grandfather had elected Hanover and paid his expenses—up to five dollars a week. But later he himself had selected Harvard because he wanted to please the memory of his father.

The years at Harvard from 1936 to 1943 were rich in publication. Whether those published poems were in any appreciable degree written in the Cambridge Interval, we cannot be sure. So far as we know, the poet has never cleared up the question. There are a few poems which have all the earmarks of the period. Some he has even dated—as "November," in *A Witness Tree,* 1938. But even this has an atmosphere of early composition, reminding one somewhat of "Nothing Gold Can Stay." But the whipcracker at the end, the powerful last line,

> The waste of nations warring,

seems to suggest the opening days of World War II.

Certain poems, such as the one first printed in the *Old Farmer's Almanac,* entitled "Rich in Stones" (changed in *A*

CAMBRIDGE INTERVAL 35

Witness Tree to "Of the Stones of the Place"), might have been thought out at Derry, or at South Shaftsbury. In the "Stones" poem, Ripton is suggested in a number of ways.

But we are more concerned here with publication. A new book was in the making, and the poet ran true to form. He bombarded the magazines. The six-year silence was broken at last when he published "Neither Out Far nor In Deep" in the *Yale Review* for spring, 1934, simultaneously publishing "Desert Places" in the *American Mercury,* and "On the Heart's Beginning to Cloud the Mind" in *Scribner's Magazine,* both appearing in April. *Scribner's* repeated in August, *New Frontier* had one in September, and the *Yale Review* used three in its autumn number. At the year's end *Scribner's* had a poem in its December number.

In 1935 he continued with two poems. The book was due the following year, and, if we count the different poems in "Ten Mills" which appeared in *Poetry: A Magazine of Verse* as entities, the year 1936 was the most productive in his literary career, with twenty-three published poems.

All these poems from 1934 through 1936 found a place in *A Further Range,* which won the Pulitzer Prize.

For a year after *A Further Range* appeared, Frost published nothing in magazines. That was 1937. In September, 1938, two of his poems appeared in the *Atlantic Monthly;* in 1939, one each in the *Atlantic Monthly* and the *Virginia Quarterly Review.* In 1941 he published three poems, and four in 1942—the year *A Witness Tree* was issued.

All in all, the Cambridge Interval, only one-third as long, rivaled the Amherst for publication if not production.

HANOVER INTERVAL
1943–

IT IS too early to ascertain the output of the poetry of Robert Frost in the Hanover Interval. All that may definitely be said is that during these years he has been writing and rewriting with painstaking care.

Published poems have been few. In 1943 an exhibition of Frost's work was shown at the Baker Library, Dartmouth. At that time a brochure was prepared, which was published in the spring of 1944, edited by Ray Nash. This contained the first printing of the poem, "Once Down on My Knees."

A hiatus of two years followed. In 1946, three poems—"Directive," "The Middleness of the Road," and "Astrometaphysical"—were published in the winter number of the *Virginia Quarterly Review.*

In November, 1946, appeared the Robert Frost number of the *New Hampshire Troubadour,* a creditable attempt at making known a poet who should already be known but who is incredibly unknown to many. Here appeared for the first time the poem, "Our Getaway."

The *Yale Review,* in its autumn number, 1946, printed "Nocturnes," which was made up of three poems: "The Night Light," "Were I in Trouble with Night To-night," and "Bravery."

The appearance of a group of seven poems in the December, 1946, *Atlantic* ("Something for Hope," "Haec Fabula Docet," "A Rogers Group," "The Ingenuities of Debt," "U.S.

HANOVER INTERVAL

1946 King's X," "The Planners," "To an Ancient") indicated, one hoped, a new book in the making; and a further indication was the appearance in the same magazine for April, 1947, of another group of four poems ("No Holy Wars for Them," "The Importer," "But He Meant It," "Etherealizing").

Of book publications, or rather selections, there was no dearth. In 1943 appeared *Come In,* which contained some of Frost's finest, with biographical notes by Louis Untermeyer. This was followed (and enlarged upon) by an edition of his selected poems for the Pocket Book series in 1946, which welcomed Frost to the drugstore counters for the first time.

An outstanding event of this interval was his first appearance in the Modern Library. Late in 1946, Random House brought out an abbreviated edition of the *Collected Poems.*

This edition will bear some critical thinking. In the blurb the publishers assert that the selection of the poems for the Modern Library edition was left to the poet. As late as the close of 1946, Frost expressed his fondness again for the first poem he ever sold, "My Butterfly." However, he left it out of this book, though he had included it religiously since it was first published in book form in *A Boy's Will.*

One can understand his omitting a great many of the 262 pieces presented in the *Collected Poems* of 1939 and in *A Witness Tree.* A few of those left out (to the thinking of many critics, properly) were "The Subverted Flower," "The Armful," "Trial by Existence," "The Pauper Witch of Grafton," and "I Will Sing You One-O." Some that he deleted (should the Modern Library edition be the standard of measurement for the future) have left a void in our literature.

There is "Pan With Us," which to some has come to mean Robert Frost as no other one poem does; "In the Home Stretch," good not only for itself but for what it gives us of the author and his life; "In a Disused Graveyard," "Hillside Thaw," "A Late Walk," "Maple," "The Thatch"; and last of all, almost of greatest importance, "Wind and Window Flower." One can hardly think of the poet without thinking of these. Others, not mentioned, omitted from the Modern Library edition have likewise left gaps.

In April, 1947, Henry Holt and Company announced the eighth book of verse from Frost's pen, to be called *Steeple Bush*. It was published May 28. Here we have several poems the dates of which are clear. The agony of the great war, and the futility of the "fabled Federation of Mankind," are present. The atom bomb is treated with an irony which comes of age—not of disillusionment. Just as in *A Further Range* our poet entered the lists for the Wright Brothers as first to fly, so here he has championed another well-nigh forgotten underdog; a note on the poem "In the Long Night" says: "Etookashoo and Couldlooktoo accompanied Dr. Cook to the North Pole."

However few or many may have been the poems written or published by our poet in the Hanover Interval, of pieces inscribed by him and sent forth from "the Golden Room" (thanks to the good offices of his colleague, Earl Cranston) there has been no want. The collection has been much enriched in these years by his painstaking comments glossed on book and magazine—enriched far more than the poet dreamed, or the collector hoped.

Bibliography

POEMS
With some reviews, articles, and other related items

Lawrence Interval
1894

"My Butterfly: An Elegy," *Independent,* November 8, 1894, p. 1. (First appearance in a book, in *A Boy's Will,* 1913.)* Inscribed: "To Louis Mertins: Kay Morrison found it for you. These were the lines that set me on my way. That's why I kept the poem in my first book. R.F."

Derry Interval
1901

"The Quest of the Orchis," *Independent,* June 27, 1901, p. 1494. (First separate appearance, in *Three Poems,* 1935; first appearance in a book, in *A Witness Tree,* 1942, under the title, "The Quest of the Purple-Fringed.")† Inscribed: "I had almost forgotten this when I came on it a few years back and put it into one of my later books. This R. L. Frost sounds like a stranger to me. Doesn't he to you Louis?"

---

* Below, where a book title and a date appear in parentheses, it is to be understood that "first appearance in a book" is thus indicated.

† Similarly, where two titles and dates appear in parentheses, the first indicates "first separate appearance," and the second, "first appearance in a book."

1906

"The Trial by Existence," *Independent,* October 11, 1906, p. 876. (*A Boy's Will,* 1913.) Inscribed: "No, I didn't have any relative in mind. R.F."

1907

"A Line-storm Song," *New England Magazine,* October, 1907, p. 204. (*A Boy's Will,* 1913.) Inscribed: "Look again. To be found in my collected. Robert Frost."

1908

"Across the Atlantic," *Independent,* March 26, 1908, p. 676. Inscribed: "Negligible Accident R.F."

1909

"Into Mine Own," *New England Magazine,* May, 1909, p. 338. (*A Boy's Will,* 1913, entitled "Into My Own.") Inscribed: "Robert Frost to Louis Mertins."

"The Flower Boat," *Youth's Companion,* May 20, 1909, p. 248. (*West-running Brook,* 1928.) Inscribed: "Robert Frost to Louis Mertins."

Dymock Interval

1912

"My November Guest," *Forum,* November, 1912, p. 612. (*A Boy's Will,* 1913.) Inscribed: "Dear Louis: You say this was the twelfth poem I sold to a magazine. I suppose you have counted them. I take your word for it.—R." (The four not included above are very rare Frost items.)

1913

Review of *A Boy's Will* by Ezra Pound, in *Poetry: A Magazine of Verse*, May, 1913, p. 72. Inscribed: (p. 72) "Poor old Ezra. As he seems now in 1944"; (p. 74) "Not true. R.F." "Ezra did this sort of thing badly. Poor Ezra."

Ticket of admission to the Poetry Bookshop, 1913, inserted in *Poetry and Drama*, December, 1913. (In 1913, at the Poetry Bookshop, Frost met influential literary men of London.) Inscribed: "Visaed—R.F: 1945 Hanover N H."

"The Fear," *Poetry and Drama*, December, 1913, p. 406. (*North of Boston*, 1914.) Inscribed: "Robert Frost to Louis Mertins."

"A Hundred Collars," *Poetry and Drama*, December, 1913, p. 409. (*North of Boston*, 1914.) Inscribed: "Robert Frost to Louis Mertins."

1914

"The Code—Heroics," *Poetry: A Magazine of Verse*, February, 1914, p. 167. (*North of Boston*, 1914.) Inscribed: "Robert Frost to Louis Mertins exactly thirty years after."

Review of *North of Boston*—"Simplicity and Sophistication"—by Wilfrid Wilson Gibson, *Bookman* (London), July, 1914, p. 183. Inscribed: "Nope I never saw it before R.F."

Review of *North of Boston*—"Modern Georgics"—by Ezra Pound, *Poetry: A Magazine of Verse*, December, 1914, p. 127. Inscribed: "N.G. says R F."

Four poems: "The Sound of Trees," "The Cow in Apple Time," "Putting in the Seed," and "The Smile," *Poetry and Drama,* December, 1914, pp. 348–349. (*Mountain Interval,* 1916, "The Sound of Trees," entitled "The Sound of the Trees," and "The Smile" made the third part of "The Hill Wife.") Inscribed (p. 349): "You ask if any of these are English in spirit. That would not be for me but for someone else to say. R.F."

1915

Review of *North of Boston* by Amy Lowell, *New Republic,* February 20, 1915, p. 81. Inscribed: "This was the first real review in America R.F."

Review of *North of Boston*—"The Tragedy of Loneliness," *Independent,* May 31, 1915, p. 368. Initialed: "R.F."

Article, "Discovered in England—A Real American Poet," with photograph, *Current Opinion,* June, 1915, p. 427. Photograph initialed: "R.F."

A group of poems: "Birches," "The Road Not Taken," and "The Sound of Trees," *Atlantic Monthly,* August, 1915, pp. 221–224. (*Mountain Interval,* 1916.) Inscribed (p. 221) on the poem "Birches": "This poem got its start here. It has gone further than most of mine. R.F."

A group of poems (second copy): "Birches," "The Road Not Taken," and "The Sound of Trees," *Atlantic Monthly,* August, 1915, pp. 221–224. (*Mountain Interval,* 1916.) Inscribed (p. 221): "I think this was the first publication of all these poems. I should have been in trouble before this if it wasn't. Robert Frost."

Review of *North of Boston* and *A Boy's Will,* together, by William Dean Howells, in "Editor's Easy Chair,"

Harper's Magazine, September, 1915, p. 634. Inscribed: "I never read this R.F."

Amherst Interval
1916

Article, "Robert Frost, a Poet of Speech," by George H. Browne, *Independent,* May 22, 1916, p. 283.

"My Butterfly," *Independent,* May 22, 1916 (reprint from issue of November 8, 1894), p. 283. (*A Boy's Will,* 1913.) Signed: "Robert Frost."

"The Vanishing Red," *Craftsman,* July, 1916, p. 383. (*Mountain Interval,* 1916.) Inscribed: "The place was Acton Mass a hundred or more years ago. This is not intended for any kind of verse. It wanted to scan but I refused to let it. R.F. 1945."

"In the Home Stretch," *Century Magazine,* July, 1916, p. 383. (*Mountain Interval,* 1916.) Inscribed: "The places resemble neither the Derry nor the Franconia farm in any least detail—says Robert Frost to Louis Mertins on October 26 1944."

Two poems: "The Telephone" and "The Gum-Gatherer," *Independent,* October 9, 1916, p. 70. (*Mountain Interval,* 1916.) Signed: "Robert Frost."

"The Bonfire," *Seven Arts,* November, 1916, p. 25. (*Mountain Interval,* 1916.) Inscribed: "Yes Derry was where I got the scare about a grassfire. I've had a worse one since in Ripton. R.F."

"An Encounter," *Atlantic Monthly,* November, 1916, p. 623. (*Mountain Interval,* 1916.) Signed: "Robert Frost."

"Snow," *Poetry: A Magazine of Verse,* November, 1916, p. 57. (*Mountain Interval,* 1916.) Inscribed: "This was when Harriet had forgiven me her mistake of not having discovered me herself R.F."

Review of *Mountain Interval*—"The Poetry of Robert Frost"—by Padraic Colum, *New Republic,* December 23, 1916, p. 219. Inscribed: "Not read but visaed R.F."

1917

Review of *Mountain Interval* by H. M., *Poetry: A Magazine of Verse,* January, 1917, p. 202. Inscribed: "XXX."

"Not to Keep," *Yale Review,* January, 1917, p. 400. (*New Hampshire,* 1923; *A Treasury of War Poetry,* 1917.) Inscribed: "This and The Bonfire were my most ostensible war poems. R.F." "To Louis Mertins."

"Not to Keep," *A Treasury of War Poetry,* Houghton Mifflin, Boston and New York, p. 219. Inscribed: "Robert Frost to Louis Mertins."

"The Axe-Helve," *Atlantic Monthly,* September, 1917, p. 337. (*New Hampshire,* 1923.) Inscribed: "The Bonfire was to have been used here. There was some sort of mix up with the editor."

1920

"To E.T.," *Yale Review,* April, 1920, p. 555. (*New Hampshire,* 1923.) Inscribed: "The second stanza comes back oftenest."

Article, "Covered Roads," by Lola Ridge, *New Republic,* June 23, 1920, pp. 131–132. Inscribed (p. 132): "Visaed R.F."

A group of poems: "Fragmentary Blue," "Place for a Third," "Good-Bye and Keep Cold," and "For Once, Then, Something," *Harper's Magazine,* July, 1920, pp. 196–199. (*New Hampshire,* 1923.) Inscribed (p. 196): "Sounds like a revival. R.F."

A group of poems: "Fire and Ice," "Wild Grapes," "The Valley's Singing Day," and "The Need of Being Versed in Country Things," *Harper's Magazine,* December, 1920, pp. 66–70. (*New Hampshire,* 1923.) Inscribed (p. 67): "Joseph Anthony came after these and gave me a fresh send off with the magazine public. R.F."

1921

A group of poems: "Snow Dust," "The Onset," "A Star in a Stone-Boat," and "Misgiving," *Yale Review,* January, 1921, pp. 258–261. (*New Hampshire,* 1923, "Snow Dust" entitled "Dust of Snow.") Inscribed (p. 258): "Robert Frost to Louis Mertins."

"A Brook in the City," *New Republic,* March 9, 1921, p. 48. (*New Hampshire,* 1923.) Inscribed: "Brook I knew of in Lawrence and one I heard of in New York Robert Frost."

"Blue-Butterfly Day," *New Republic,* March 16, 1921, p. 74. (*New Hampshire,* 1923.) Signed: "Robert Frost."

Two poems: "The Census Taker" and "A Hillside Thaw," *New Republic,* April 6, 1921, p. 161. (*New Hampshire,* 1923.) Inscribed: "Robert Frost for Louis Mertins."

"The Pauper Witch of Grafton," *Nation,* April 13, 1921, Spring Book Supplement, p. 549. (*New Hampshire,* 1923.) Inscribed: "Robert Frost to Louis Mertins."

"Maple," *Yale Review*, October, 1921, p. 52. (*New Hampshire*, 1923.) Inscribed: "By Robert Frost."

"Paul's Wife," *Century Magazine*, November, 1921, p. 83. (*New Hampshire*, 1923.) Inscribed (p. 84): "Robert Frost to Louis Mertins"; on photograph [p. viii]: "When I was young. R.F."

"Paul's Wife" (second copy), *Century Magazine*, November, 1921, p. 83. (*New Hampshire*, 1923.) Inscribed (p. 84): "by Robert Frost."

1922

"The Witch of Coos," *Poetry: A Magazine of Verse*, January, 1922, p. 175. (*New Hampshire*, 1923.) Inscribed: "Robert Frost to Louis Mertins."

1923

"Stopping by Woods on a Snowy Evening," *New Republic*, March 7, 1923, p. 47. (*New Hampshire*, 1923.) Inscribed: "Why, why! I had forgotten this. R.F." Manuscript of this poem in Carnegie Library at William Jewell College, Liberty, Missouri, inscribed: "For my poet friend Marshall Louis Mertins, Robert Frost."

"Our Singing Strength," *New Republic*, May 2, 1923, p. 264. (*New Hampshire*, 1923.) Inscribed: "Robert Frost to Louis Mertins 1945."

"The Star-Splitter," *Century Magazine*, September, 1923, p. 681. (*New Hampshire*, 1923.) Inscribed (p. 682): "Robert Frost 1945"; under portrait of Alexander Meiklejohn [p. viii]: "Who first called me to be a professor R.F."

"The Star-Splitter" (second copy), *Century Magazine*, September, 1923, p. 681. (*New Hampshire,* 1923.) Inscribed: "October 1945 There ought to be one now on the atom-splitter R F. Robert Frost to Louis Mertins."

"A Fountain, a Bottle, a Donkey's Ears and Some Books," *Bookman,* October, 1923, p. 121. (*New Hampshire,* 1923.) Signed: "Robert Frost."

"Gathering Leaves," *Current Opinion,* October, 1923, p. 479. (*New Hampshire,* 1923.) Inscribed: "R.F. Meeting this for the first time."

Three poems: "Nothing Gold Can Stay," "To Earthward," and "I Will Sing You One-O," *Yale Review,* October, 1923, pp. 30–33. (*New Hampshire,* 1923.) Inscribed (p 30): "Robert Frost to Louis Mertins."

"A Boundless Moment," *New Republic,* October 24, 1923, p. 223. (*New Hampshire,* 1923.) Signed: "Robert Frost."

"Stopping by Woods on a Snowy Evening," *Best Poems of 1923,* Small-Maynard, Boston, p. 88. Inscribed: "Robert Frost 45 with the same friendship as when I signed it for L.M. in 1932."

1924

"Lodged," *New Republic,* February 6, 1924, p. 281. (*West-running Brook,* 1928.) Inscribed: "Ripton Vt 1945 Interesting to know I sometimes felt this way as early as thirty years ago when this was written R.F."

"Mending Wall," *Poems of Today,* Ginn, Boston, p. 119. Signed: "Robert Frost."

1926

A poem about Robert Frost, "The Golden Room," by Wilfrid Gibson, *Atlantic Monthly,* February, 1926, p. 204.

Inscribed: "Since Louis wants me to say I have seen it. Robert Frost." This magazine came from England in 1943, signed and corrected (spelling of Elinor Frost) in Wilfrid Gibson's hand. It was in an accident and lime juice was spilled on it in transit, almost blotting out Gibson's signature.

A poem about Robert Frost, "The Golden Room," by Wilfrid Gibson (second copy), *Atlantic Monthly*, February, 1926, p. 204. Inscribed: "L.M., I owe Wilfrid Gibson much kindness for so much kindness don't I? R.F."

Holograph manuscript, "The Golden Room," by Wilfrid Gibson, signed by Wilfrid Gibson. Inscribed: "We must admit this was terribly nice of Wilfred [*sic*]. He and I were neighbors away down in the country in 1913–14. I wonder how you found this copy of his poem all done out in his hand Robert Frost to Louis Mertins April 20, 1945."

"The Passing Glimpse," *New Republic*, April 21, 1926, p. 275. (*West-running Brook*, 1928.) Inscribed: "One of my greatest friends. R.F." (Ridgely Torrence.)

"Sand Dunes," *New Republic*, December 15, 1926, p. 111. (*West-running Brook*, 1928.) Inscribed: "Robert Frost 1945."

"The Same Leaves," *Dearborn Independent*, December 18, 1926, p. 2 of cover. (*Collected Poems*, 1930, entitled "In Hardwood Groves.") Inscribed: "R.F Oct 1945."

Article, "Robert Frost's Hilltop," by Dorothy Canfield Fisher, *Bookman*, December, 1926, p. 403. Inscribed: "Years ago, when Sarah Cleghorn, a Vermont poet—and a good one—first read Robert Frost's poems, she said 'Oh, what's the use of anybody else trying to write New England poetry. Robert Frost says, perfectly, totally, what we all want said'. That's what I think, too. Dorothy Canfield Fisher"; "Dorothy was always a good neighbor as the above shows Robert Frost"; "When I saw this pasture ten years later I couldn't recognize it for the trees. J J L." Lankes' inscription refers to his picture of Robert Frost's Vermont Pasture on p. 405.

Article, "Robert Frost's Hilltop," by Dorothy Canfield Fisher (second copy), *Bookman,* December, 1926, p. 403. Inscribed: "You can see my favorite *tool* (my pen is a weapon) hanging on the porch. R.F. 1944." Refers to Lankes' picture of the Frost homestead on p. 403.

"Once by the Pacific," *New Republic,* December 29, 1926, p. 156. (*West-running Brook,* 1928.) Inscribed: "One of my few Californian R.F."

Essay, "Robert Frost," by Gorman B. Munson, *Current Reviews,* Holt, New York, 1926, p. 319. Inscribed: "This began my friendship for Gorham [*sic*] B. R.F."

1927

"A Winter Eden," *New Republic,* January 12, 1927, p. 215. (*West-running Brook,* 1928.) Inscribed: "Robert Frost Interesting to meet these old ones again."

Three poems: "The Cocoon," "The Times Table," and "Bereft," *New Republic,* February 9, 1927, p. 327. (*West-running Brook,* 1928.) Inscribed: "Signed Robert Frost for Louis Mertins."

"Spring Pools," *Dearborn Independent,* April 23, 1927, p. 2 of cover. (*West-running Brook,* 1928.) Signed: "Robert Frost."

"The Cow's in the Corn," *Dearborn Independent,* June 18, 1927, p. 2 of cover. Inscribed: "Don't remember ever having seen this before. R.F. Oct 1945."

Four poems: "Tree at My Window," "The Minor Bird," "The Rose Family," and "The Common Fate," *Yale Review,* July, 1927, pp. 657–659. (*West-running Brook,* 1928.) Inscribed (p. 657): "For Louis Mertins Robert Frost."

1928

"The Armful," *Nation,* February 8, 1928, p. 151. (*West-running Brook,* 1928.) Initialed: "R.F."

"Blood," *Nation,* February 8, 1928, p. 151. (*West-running Brook,* 1928, entitled "The Flood." For the change from "Blood" to "Flood" we have as yet no explanation.) Inscribed: "R.L.F. Reaffirmed in 1945."

"The Bear," *Nation,* April 18, 1928, Spring Book Section, p. 447. (*West-running Brook,* 1928.) Signed: "Robert Frost."

Article, "Robert Frost," in the Poetry Corner, edited by Orton Lowe, *Scholastic,* September 22, 1928, p. 13; poems: "The Need of Being Versed in Country Things" and "The Runaway," *Amherst Monthly,* June, 1918, p. 51. (*New Hampshire,* 1923.) Inscribed: "Robert Frost."

"Acquainted with the Night," *Virginia Quarterly Review,* October, 1928, p. 541. (*West-running Brook,* 1928.) Signed: "Robert Frost."

"Inscription for a Garden Wall," *Ladies' Home Journal,*

October, 1928, p. 17. (*West-running Brook,* 1928, entitled "Atmosphere.") Inscribed: "Permission to Plaque. Robert Frost."

1931

Article, "Robert Frost: American Poet," by James Southall Wilson, *Virginia Quarterly Review,* April, 1931, p. 316. Inscribed: "Seen in California. R.F."

1932

Untitled poem ("Reluctance"), *Golden Book Magazine,* January, 1932, p. 5. (*Youth's Companion,* November 7, 1912, p. 612; *A Boy's Will,* 1913.) Inscribed: "R.F. to L.M Oct 1945."

First printing of Frost's letter to Mencken concerning censorship of Dreiser's book, in *Forgotten Frontiers,* by Dorothy Dudley, Smith and Haas, New York, 1932, p. 367. Initialed: "R.F."

1934

"Neither Out Far nor In Deep," *Yale Review,* spring, 1934, p. 484. (*A Further Range,* 1936.) Inscribed: "This was one of my few Californian poems. But it is made of mixed memories. Take care of the MS of it I gave you Louis. R.F." The prepublication draft of the manuscript appears on the blank last page of *A Lone Striker.*

"Desert Places," *American Mercury,* April, 1934, p. 464. (*A Further Range,* 1936.) Inscribed: "Robert Frost New England 1944."

"On the Heart's Beginning to Cloud the Mind," *Scribner's Magazine,* April, 1934, p. 286. (*A Further Range,* 1936.)

Inscribed: "I wrote this in a hotel in Wilkesbarre Pennsylvania. R F."

"They Were Welcome to Their Belief," *Scribner's Magazine,* August, 1934, p. 86. (*A Further Range,* 1936.) Inscribed: "Robert Frost to Louis Mertins."

"Provide Provide," *New Frontier,* September, 1934, p. 11. (*A Further Range,* 1936.) Inscribed: "Robert Frost to Louis Mertins."

Three poems: "Moon Compasses," "A Missive Missile," and "After-Flakes," *Yale Review,* autumn, 1934, pp. 34–36. (*A Further Range,* 1936.) Inscribed (p. 34): "L.M. I believe I wrote the third of these in California when we were round together. R.F."

"Neither Out Far nor In Deep," in "A Sheaf of Verse," by Louis Mertins, *Citizen,* December 7, 1934. Inscribed: "Pleasure to make this over to you a second time Louis. R.F. New England 1944." This is the first printing of the original draft.

"On a Bird Singing in Its Sleep," *Scribner's Magazine,* December, 1934, p. 344. (*A Further Range,* 1936.) Inscribed: "Robert Frost New England 1944."

1935

"Not Quite Social," *Saturday Review of Literature,* March 30, 1935, p. 578. (*A Further Range,* 1936.) Inscribed: "Robert Frost 1945."

"A Leaf-Treader," *American Mercury,* October, 1935, p. 142. (*A Further Range,* 1936.) Inscribed: "Robert Frost New England 1944."

Four poems: "Departmental," "Voice-Ways," "Master Speed," and "The Bearer of Evil Tidings," *Yale Review*, December, 1935, pp. 217–220. (*A Further Range*, 1936.) Inscribed (p. 217): "Robert Frost to Louis Mertins."

1936

Three poems: "Iris by Night," "The Figure in the Doorway," and "In Time of Cloudburst," *Virginia Quarterly Review*, April, 1936, pp. 232–234. (*A Further Range*, 1936.) Signed (p. 233): "Robert Frost." Frost has underscored "if so moved" in the last line of "The Figure in the Doorway."

"The White-tailed Hornet or Doubts about an Instinct," *Yale Review*, spring, 1936, p. 459. (*A Further Range*, 1936, entitled "The White-tailed Hornet.") Inscribed: "Robert Frost to Louis Mertins."

"A Blue Ribbon at Amesbury," *Atlantic Monthly*, April 1936, pp. 420–421. (*A Further Range*, 1936.) Inscribed (p. 421): "You ask was this in Derry. How can you ask, Louis?—R.F."

Two poems: "At Woodward's Gardens" and "Ten Mills," *Poetry: A Magazine of Verse*, April, 1936, pp. 1–5. (*A Further Range*, 1936.) Inscribed (p. 3): "For Louis Mertins from R.F."; (p. 4, "Untried"): "You had this in MS before it was printed."

"Name Unnamed," the manuscript of a poem [entitled "Untried" in *Poetry: A Magazine of Verse*, April, 1936, and "Waspish" in *A Further Range*, 1936]. Initialed: "R.F."

"The Strong Are Saying Nothing," *American Mercury*, May, 1936, p. 58. (*A Further Range*, 1936.) Inscribed: "Robert Frost October 1944."

"A Record Stride," *Atlantic Monthly*, May, 1936, p. 593. (*A Further Range*, 1936.) Inscribed: "Robert Frost." Opposite the first stanza he has written, "South Shaftsbury." In the fourth stanza he has underscored the words Cliff House and has written opposite, "or Long Beach rather."

Article, "Wise Old Woodchuck," by William Rose Benét, *Saturday Review of Literature*, May 30, 1936, p. 6. Signed, under engraving by J. J. Lankes: "Robert Frost"; on portrait on cover: "Robert Frost."

Poems in a Time of Doubt: "A Roadside Stand," "A Drumlin Woodchuck," and "A Trial Run," *Atlantic Monthly*, June, 1936, pp. 669–671. (*A Further Range*, 1936.) Inscribed (p. 671): "Robert Frost to Louis Mertins."

Robert Frost: A Chronological Survey, Library, Middletown, Connecticut, 1936, includes the first printing of an early draft of "Nothing Gold Can Stay," p. 30. Inscribed (under portrait): "Robert Frost to Louis Mertins."

Cambridge Interval

1937

"Blueberries" (partial), *Old Farmer's Almanac*, 1937, p. 21. Signed: "Robert Frost."

"Neither Out Far nor In Deep," *Contemporary American Men Poets*, Harrison, New York, p. 147. Inscribed: "R.F. to L.M. to remind him of the day we went down the coast together."

Recognition of Robert Frost, Holt, New York, 1937. Signed (under portrait): "Robert Frost."

Robert Frost and the Sound of Sense, by Robert S. Newdick, 1937 (reprinted from *American Literature,* November, 1937). Inscribed (cover title page under Newdick's by-line): "My friend. R.F."; (cover title page in Newdick's hand, not signed, "for Miss Sylvia Clark").

Some Notes on Robert Frost and Shakespere, by Robert S. Newdick, 1937 (reprinted from the Shakespeare Association *Bulletin,* July, 1937). Inscribed: "Sylvia Clark was my fellow teacher at Pinkerton Academy. Newdick was to have been my biographer. He had done but a few chapters about me before he died. He was still very young. R.F." (Inscribed by Newdick on cover title: "for Sylvia Clark with kindest regard Robert S. Newdick"; and after the date, July, 1937, "but just received!")

Robert Frost: A Bibliography, by W. B. Shubrick Clymer and Charles R. Green, The Jones Library, Inc., Amherst, Massachusetts, 1937. Inscribed (end paper): "To Louis Mertins from Robert Frost and Kathleen Morrison (it was her copy) December 1941 Cambridge Massachusetts."

1938

Two poems: "Carpe Diem" and "Happiness Makes Up in Height for What It Lacks in Length," *Atlantic Monthly,* September, 1938, pp. 316–317. (*A Witness Tree,* 1942.) Inscribed (p. 317): "Robert Frost to Louis Mertins 1944."

1939

Review of *Collected Poems*, in *Time*, May 15, 1939, p. 83. Initialed (portrait, p. 84): "R.F."

"A Considerable Speck," *Atlantic Monthly*, July, 1939, p. 47. (*A Witness Tree*, 1942, entitled "A Considerable Speck (Microscopic).") Inscribed: "Robert Frost 1944."

"The Silken Tent," *Virginia Quarterly Review*, winter, 1939, p. 20. (*A Witness Tree*, 1942.) Inscribed: "Robert Frost to Louis Mertins."

1940

A Chat with Robert Frost, by Cyril Clemens, International Mark Twain Society, Webster Groves, Missouri, 1940. Inscribed (title page): "Robert Frost who didn't know what to think of this." (Signed by Cyril Clemens.)

1941

"Come In," *Atlantic Monthly*, February, 1941, p. 145. (*A Witness Tree*, 1942.) Inscribed: "Robert Frost to Louis Mertins."

"Come In" (second copy), *Atlantic Monthly*, February, 1941 p. 145. (*A Witness Tree*, 1942.) Signed: "Robert Frost."

"The Literate Farmer and the Planet Venus," *Atlantic Monthly*, March, 1941, p. 284. (*A Witness Tree*, 1942.) Inscribed: "Just to think of it! I had read this to Louis Mertins ten years before I sent it to be printed. R.F."

"I Could Give All to Time," *Yale Review*, autumn, 1941, p. 24. (*A Witness Tree*, 1942.) Signed: "Robert Frost."

1942

"Rich in Stones," *Old Farmer's Almanac,* 1942, p. 2. (*A Witness Tree,* 1942, entitled "Of the Stones of the Place.") Inscribed: "To Louis Mertins from Robert Frost."

Three poems: "Time Out," "To a Moth Seen in Winter," and "The Gift Outright," *Virginia Quarterly Review,* spring, 1942, pp. 240–242. (*A Witness Tree,* 1942.) Inscribed (p. 241): "You can't get me to believe this happened in Derry. R.F."

Review of *A Witness Tree,* in *Time,* May 18, 1942, pp. 91–92. Inscribed (p. 92): "Robert Frost."

Review of *A Witness Tree* by Louis Mertins, *Southern Literary Messenger,* July, 1942, p. 327. Inscribed: "Thanks to Louis for all this kindness. R.F. 1945."

"Some Woodcuts of J. J. Lankes & Some Talk of Robert Frost," *The Month at Goodspeed's,* January, 1943, pp. 86–89. Inscribed (p. 87): "J J has been one of my greatest friends all the years R F to L M." Inscribed by Lankes, p. 86: "I've never called myself Mr. J. J. Lankes"; front cover, "Signed for Louis Mertins J. J. Lankes"; back cover, "My father's grindstone. J. J. L."

Hanover Interval

1943

"In the Long Night," early draft manuscript of this poem. Inscribed: "Robert Frost to Louis Mertins Christmas War-times 1943."

1944

"In the Long Night," first appearance of this poem in print, in *Dartmouth in Portrait* (Dartmouth College, Hanover, New Hampshire, 1944). *Dartmouth in Portrait* is a calendar containing selections from Frost's poems. Its frontispiece is a portrait of Frost by Emile Rueb. Inscribed (p. 3, at poem): "Robert Frost to Louis Mertins"; (p. 1, under portrait): "Robert Frost to Louis Mertins."

Fifty Years of Robert Frost, edited by Ray Nash, Dartmouth College Library, Hanover, New Hampshire, 1944. Includes first printing of poem "Once Down on My Knees," p. 13. Inscribed: "Robert Frost to Louis Mertins."

Portrait (from the painting by Keith Martin), *Saturday Review of Literature,* August 5, 1944, p. 18. Initialed: "R F."

1946

Three poems: "Directive," "The Middleness of the Road," and "Astrometaphysical," *Virginia Quarterly Review,* winter, 1946, pp. 1–4. Inscribed (p. 1): "Robert Frost to Louis Mertins."

"The Constant Symbol" (prose), *Atlantic Monthly,* October, 1946, p. 50. (*The Poems of Robert Frost,* 1946.) Inscribed: "Robert Frost to Louis Mertins."

The New Hampshire Troubadour, Robert Frost Issue, November, 1946, includes first printing of "Our Getaway," p. 9; articles on Frost by West, Poole, Morse, Clark, Cox, Bartlett, and Lambuth. Inscribed (p. 9): "Robert Frost." Frost crossed out the phrase after the comma in line 5 of "Our Getaway," "and to what better show," and all of line 6, "By whose space rocket we expect to steer," substituting "will she be asked to show / Us how by rocket we may hope to steer."

(Three) "Nocturnes": "The Night Light," "Were I in Trouble with Night To-night," and "Bravery," *Yale Review*, autumn, 1946, p. 37. Inscribed: "Robert Frost to Louis Mertins."

Seven poems: "Something for Hope," "Haec Fabula Docet," "A Rogers Group," "The Ingenuities of Debt," "U. S. 1946 King's X," "The Planners," "To an Ancient," *Atlantic Monthly*, December, 1946, pp. 50–53.

1947

Article, "Robert Frost Speaks to Students," by Ruth Ray, *Daily Californian*, March 26, 1947, p. 6. Initialed: "R.F."

Four poems: "No Holy Wars for Them," "The Importer," "But He Meant It," "Etherealizing," *Atlantic Monthly*, April, 1947, pp. 54–55.

MARGINALIA

Bibliographical and biographical items with marginal notes in Robert Frost's hand:

The Parable of Creation, John Doughty, 1892.
Notebook of Pinkerton student. N.d. (*ca.* 1906).
Grocery list, Monrovia, California, 1932.
List of guests, organization meeting, California Writers' Guild, Occidental College, California, 1932.

Photographs:

    Robert Frost at Occidental (frontispiece), 1932.
    Robert Frost at Laguna, California (two copies), 1932.
    Robert Frost at Ripton, Vermont, 1942 (*sic*).
    Robert Frost at Miami, Florida, 1942.
    Derry Farmhouse, from northwest.
    Derry Farmhouse, from southwest.
    Stone Wall at Derry.
    Orchard at Derry.
    Woods at Derry.
    "Road Not Taken," Derry.
    "Tree at My Window," Derry.
    Frost's log cabin at Ripton, 1940 (*sic*).
    Frost's garden at Ripton, 1941.

Silhouettes:

    Robert Frost as a young man.
    Robert Frost (*ca.* 1940).
    Drawing by Olive Spittler (*ca.* 1932).

Publisher's announcement of *A Further Range* (*ca.* 1936).
Program of Little Theatre, Bread Loaf, August 10, 1941.
The George Matthew Adams Vachel Lindsay Collection, Dartmouth College Library, Hanover, N. H., 1945.
Typed list of Frostana advertised by the American Library Service, New York [1942].

BOOKS

A Boy's Will

FIRST EDITION, FOURTH ISSUE, 1913

This is the first printing, which was bound and issued in four separate forms, of which this is the last. Bound in cream-colored paper. The title page bears the following:

A Boy's Will / by / Robert Frost / London / David Nutt / 17 Grape Street, New Oxford Street, W.C. / 1913

Page next after title has rubber stamp: Printed in Great Britain.

Page 50 bears the legend: Printed by / Spottiswoode and Co. Ltd., Colchester / London and Eton.

Page 52 bears the advertisement of Nutt's 1s. Series of Modern Poets.

The first and second issues may be distinguished from the others by the fact that pages 2 and 3 in the table of contents are incorrectly numbered. The first issue was bound in brown pebbled cloth, the second in cream vellum boards, the third and fourth heavy cream-colored paper. The third may be distinguished from the fourth by the lettering on the binding, which is similar to that on the first and second but different from that on the fourth.

Inscription (on half title): To Louis Mertins from Robert Frost.

North of Boston
First edition, fifth issue [1914]

This is the first printing, which was issued in six forms, of which this is the last but one. Bound in light green buckram, ruled at top and bottom instead of all round. The title page bears the following:

North of Boston / by / Robert Frost / Author of "A Boy's Will" / London / David Nutt / 17 Grape Street / New Oxford Street / Editorial: / 6 Bloomsbury Street / W.C. (A vertical line divides the addresses.)

Page following title bears line: First edition, 1914, with rubber stamp: Printed in Great Britain.

Page 144 bears printer's legend: Printed by Ballantyne, Hanson & Co. / at Paul's Work, Edinburgh.

Nearly all the various issues may be distinguished by the binding. The first issue was bound in green buckram with blind rule, lettered in gold; the second, in light tan paper-covered boards; the third, in green buckram not printed in gilt; the fourth, in light blue linen; the fifth, likewise; and the sixth like the fifth except that the pages measure $5\frac{3}{8} \times 7\frac{3}{4}$ inches.

Inscription (on half title):

> I thought that only
> Some one who lived in turning to fresh tasks
> Could so forget his handiwork on which
> He spent himself the labor of his ax
> And leave it there far from a useful fireplace
> To warm the frozen swamp as best it could
> With the slow smokeless burning of decay

For Louis Mertins   ROBERT FROST

On the title page Frost has written above his autograph: First Printing. R.F.

NORTH OF BOSTON

SECOND AMERICAN EDITION, 1915

This is a copy of the fourth issue of the first book of Frost's poetry to be printed from type set in America and sent forth under an American copyright. Inasmuch as the so-called "first American edition" was made from sheets shipped from London, leftovers from the first English edition, many bibliopoles and bibliographers elect to hold this as the genuine "first American edition." The title page bears the following:

North of Boston / by / Robert Frost / Author of "A Boy's Will" / [colophon] / New York / Henry Holt and Company / 1915

Inscription (on half title): To Louis Mertins from Robert Frost.

Second copy [1925]. This is a reprinting of the second American edition of *North of Boston,* which, beginning in 1921, showed the original plaster of Aroldo Du Chêne's bust of Frost as a frontispiece. The same plates were used as in the original printings of 1915. Changes include the list of printings on the verso, the binding, the enlarged dimensions of the pages, and the omission of the date and the line, Author of "A Boy's Will," from the title page. Bound in light green paper-covered boards, backstrip of slightly darker green cloth, no lines, lettered in gold on front cover and spine as in first printings.

Inscription: To Louis Mertins from Robert Frost.

A Boy's Will

FIRST AMERICAN EDITION, FIRST PRINTING, 1915

This is the issue in which the "aind" on page 14 is corrected to "and"; it is also one of the first copies, as is shown by the cream-colored end papers and the fact that the publisher's name on the spine is slightly smaller than it is on *Mountain Interval*. Later copies had brown end papers and lettering in larger type at bottom of spine. Bound in blue cloth, lettered in gilt on spine. The title page bears the following:

A Boy's Will / by /Robert Frost / Author of "North of Boston" / [colophon] / New York / Henry Holt and Company / 1915

Inscription (on half title): from Robert Frost to remind Louis Mertins of the day they rode down the coast of California together in 1932.

Second copy. Same as the first except for rebinding. Frost's picture with a group is pasted on the title page. On page 16 Frost has corrected the stanza divisions and initialed it R.F. 1941.

Inscription (on flyleaf): Visaed by Robert Frost at Ripton Vermont in August of 1941 for Louis Mertins.

Mountain Interval

FIRST EDITION, FIRST ISSUE [1916]

This is the first printing, with the repeated line 7 on page 88, line 6 being omitted—an error corrected in the second issue. It is one of the rarest of Frost's books—for which there seems to be no special explanation. Four thousand copies of the first edition were printed. The binding is similar to that of the first American edition of *A Boy's Will:* blue cloth, lettered in gilt. The dust jacket is of heavy gray paper, with an advertisement of *North of Boston* and *A Boy's Will* on the back. The title page bears the following:

Mountain Interval / by / Robert Frost / Author of "North of Boston" / [colophon] / New York / Henry Holt and Company

Inscription (on flyleaf):

> It asks of us a certain height
> So when at times the mob is swayed
> To carry praise or blame too far
> We may take something like a star
> To stay our minds on and be staid.
>
> ROBERT FROST
>
> To Louis Mertins
>   Christmas 1943

NEW HAMPSHIRE

FIRST EDITION, 1923

This is the first printing, bound in dark green paper-covered boards with a brighter green backstrip, with publisher's colophon on spine. The *S* of New Hampshire on the spine curves downward between the divided Hamp- and -hire. End papers, mottled brown. The title page reads:

New Hampshire / A Poem with Notes / and Grace Notes by / Robert Frost / with Woodcuts / by J. J. Lankes / Published by / Henry Holt / & Company: New / York: MCMXXIII

Inscription (on end paper): For Louis Mertins from Robert Frost Christmas 1941 Cambridge Mass.

(Inscription on frontispiece: How the hell does a poet make $100,000 to give away? Or is that just valuation? J. J. Lankes.)

Several Short Poems

only edition, n.d. [1924]

This is the four-page sheet printed by Henry Holt and Company for use at the Frost lectures in several colleges. None of the poems included appears here for the first time. Printed on a single sheet of grayish paper, it was folded to make four pages. Page one is the title page, and bears the following:

Several / Short Poems / by / Robert Frost / Woodcut [of grindstone] by J. J. Lankes / The Pasture / [text of poem] / Copyright by Henry Holt and Company

Page two contains: "Stopping by Woods on a Snowy Evening" and "The Oven Bird"; page three, "An Old Man's Winter Night" [ornament]; page four, "The Runaway," "Nothing Gold Can Stay." Below, an advertisement of Frost's books.

Inscription (on page one): Louis Mertins from Robert Frost.

West-running Brook

first edition [1928]

This is the printing which has the mistake (later corrected) in the final line of page 44, where "roams" occurs in place of "romps." Bound in dark green paper-covered boards with a brighter green backstrip. End papers, mottled brown. The title page bears the following:

West-running / Brook / by / Robert Frost / [colophon] / New York / Henry Holt and Company
  Inscription (on end paper):

> The discipline man needed most
> Was to learn his submission to unreason
> . . . .
> So he won't find it hard to take his orders
> From his inferiors in intelligence
> In peace and war—especially in war.
>
> So he won't find it hard to take his war.
>
> ROBERT FROST
>
> To Louis Mertins
>   December 1943

On page 19, at the picture of the sycamore, Frost has written: One of Lankes' four best. R.F.

A WAY OUT

LIMITED EDITION, 1929

This is the definitive first edition—the only time it ever appeared in an edition by itself. Bound in light orange paper-covered boards with black cloth backstrip. Lettering on spine in gold. The title page bears the following:

A Way Out / A One Act Play / by / Robert Frost / [rule] / [ornament in brown ink] / [rule] / New York / The Harbor Press / 1929
  Inscription (on end paper): To Louis Mertins from Robert Frost Christmas 1941 Cambridge Mass.

Collected Poems
FIRST EDITION, 1930

This is the Random House edition, with "laces" for "faces," page 128, line 8. Bound in light tan buckram. Brown label lettered in gilt on spine. The title page bears the following:

Robert Frost / Collected / Poems / New York / Random House / 1930

Inscription (on half title): To Louis Mertins from his friend near Boston Robert Frost November 1932.

The Augustan Books of Poetry
Robert Frost
[1932]

This is the first issue and binding of this English selection of Frost's poems. The combined title page and front cover bears the following:

The Augustan Books of / Poetry / Robert / Frost / London: Ernest Benn Ltd. / Bouverie House, Fleet Street

Inscription (on cover title): For Marshall Louis Mertins from his friend Robert Frost Monrovia California September 1932.

Second copy. Publisher's copy for Frost, bound in light gray-blue cloth with corners and backstrip in dark blue leather. Lettering in gold.

Inscription (on blue end paper): Louis Mertins from R.F.

Third copy. Same as second copy.

Inscription (on title page): Robert Frost for Louis Mertins always.

THE LONE STRIKER
FIRST EDITION, 1933

This is one of the few books published by Frost with any publisher except Holt. In *A Further Range* this poem is entitled "A Lone Striker." No title page. Cover in pinkish buff. Title and author on cover in red, engraving in black. Cover title bears the following:

The Lone Striker / [engraving] / Robert Frost

Back cover bears legend: Number eight of The Borzoi Chap Books / Published by Alfred A. Knopf, 730 Fifth Avenue, New / York. Designs by W. A. Dwiggins. Printed at the / Plimpton Press.

Front flap bears legend: Copyright 1933, By Robert Frost.

Inscription (on front flyleaf): Contents / The Lone Striker or / Without Prejudice to Anything / Neither Out Far nor In Deep.

On page four, a very early draft of "Neither Out Far nor In Deep." Three stanzas.

Inscription below the signed poem: To Louis Mertins these two poems for the many lovely ones he sent me.—R.F.

SELECTED POEMS
THIRD EDITION [1934]

As against the first (1923) edition with 41 poems, and the second (1928) with 57, the third edition offered 73. Bound in pale blue buckram; author's signature impressed on front cover in gilt; spine also stamped in gilt. Light blue end papers. The title page reads as follows.

Selected Poems / by / Robert Frost / Third Edition / [colophon] / New York / Henry Holt and Company

Inscription (on end paper): For Virginia Mertins de Vries with thanks for all the *good* things she said about my books. Robert Frost Key West Florida February 1935.

Two Tramps in Mud-time
only edition, 1934

This was used by Elinor and Robert Frost for their 1934 Christmas card. Five other persons had their own imprint on similar cards. It was later included in *A Further Range*. It had appeared in the *Saturday Review of Literature* on October 6, preceding its appearance as a Christmas card. Bound in terra-cotta paper. Blank. The title page bears the following:

Two Tramps in Mud-time / A New Poem / by Robert Frost / [star] / Sent with / Holiday Greetings / from / Elinor & Robert Frost / Christmas. 1934

On the verso of the title page is the legend: Copyright 1934 by Robert Frost.

Page seven bears the legend: Printed by the Spiral Press. New York.

Inscription (on title page): To Louis Mertins from Robert Frost Key West Florida.

The Gold Hesperidee
first edition, n.d. [1935]

This is the English (rubber stamp) first edition, of which 67 copies were issued. Note the long, awkward last line but

BIBLIOGRAPHY 71

one on page 7, which caused the publisher to withdraw the first edition as first issued, after 37 copies were released. An omission occurs on page 3, line 6, where the preposition "in" is left out before "*A Boy's Will*." The title page bears the following:

The / Gold Hesperidee / by / Robert Frost

Inscription (on end paper): To Louis Mertins from R.F.

Neither Out Far nor In Deep

only edition, 1935

This was used by Elinor and Robert Frost for their 1935 Christmas card. Eight other persons had their own imprints on similar cards. The poem had appeared in March, 1934, in the *Yale Review*. Bound in mottled Japanese paper, the cover is blank. The title page bears the following:

Neither Out Far nor In Deep / A Poem by Robert Frost / Woodcut by J. J. Lankes / [star] / Sent with Holiday Greetings / at Christmas 1935 from / Elinor & Robert Frost

The title page has a border of yellow stars, the star in the title set-up being also in yellow.

Page five bears the title Neither Out Far nor In Deep, with woodcut.

Page 8 bears the legend: Printed at The Spiral Press / [star] / Copyright 1935 by Robert Frost / [star] / Courtesy of The Yale Review

Inscription (on page one): L.M. from R.F.

A Further Range
TRADE EDITION, FIRST PRINTING [1936]

This is the first printing of the originally planned first edition which formed the so-called trade edition. Bound in red buckram, with gilt lettering on front cover and spine. The title page bears the following:

Book Six / [rule] / A / Further / Range / by / Robert / Frost / [rule] / Henry Holt and Company / New York

Inscription (on half title): [A Further Range] by Robert Frost to Louis Mertins in friendship.

A Further Range
LIMITED EDITION [1936]

This is the special limited edition which was planned for release after the trade edition but which actually came out earlier, so that it is to all intents and purposes the first edition. This the poet probably had in mind in his inscription, in which he refers to this as "my secretly published book." The binding is of coarse light tan linen mottled with brown. Brown leather strip printed in gilt on spine. The title page bears the following:

A / Further / Range / by / Robert / Frost / Book Six / [rule] / Henry Holt and Company / New York (The words Book Six are in brown, the rest in black.)

The half title bears the following: A Further Range / Eight hundred and three copies / of this book were especially printed and / bound, and signed by the author / [Robert Frost] / This copy is number / [323] (Frost has signed it and it is numbered in ink.)

Page 104 bears printer's legend: Printed at the Spiral Press New York / Completed May . 1936.

Inscription (on end paper): For Louis Mertins as a surprise, this my secretly published (as distinguished from privately printed) book about California among other places. Ever his Robert Frost Amherst Mass June 1936.

Second copy same as the foregoing, numbered 47.

Inscription (on half title): Robert Frost for Louis Mertins.

To A Young Wretch
FIRST EDITION [1937]

This is the Christmas card which used the picture by J. J. Lankes with a star similar to that in "Vermont Dawn." Bound in gilt paper, printed in black. This poem later appeared in *A Witness Tree*. The title page bears the following:

Robert Frost [dot] To a Young Wretch / [woodcut in blue ink]

On verso of title page is the legend: Copyright 1937 by Robert Frost . Amherst . Massachusetts.

Page seven bears the legend: Woodcuts by J. J. Lankes. Printed at the Spiral Press, New York.

Inscription (on end paper): To Louis Mertins from Robert Frost.

Collected Poems
FIRST HALCYON HOUSE EDITION [1939]

This is the first printing of the collected poems including *A Further Range*. The edition shows the correction in the poem "Good Hours" on page 128, where in the original *Collected* line 8 read "laces" for "faces." Otherwise no changes are apparent. Pagination is the same as that of the 1930 edition, as far as that edition went. The type is heavier though apparently the same. The book is bound in green cloth, with lettering at top of spine gold on black. On front side of cover, indented, Frost's signature. End papers. No half title. Frontispiece, Frost's portrait by Doris Ulmann. The title page bears the following:

Collected Poems of / Robert / Frost / [decoration] / Halcyon House · New York

On verso of title page: Copyright, 1930, By Henry Holt and Company, Inc. / Copyright, 1936, by Robert Frost / Halcyon House Edition, March, 1939 / Halcyon House Editions are published and / distributed by Blue Ribbon Books, Inc., / 14 West 49th Street, New York City / CL / Printed in the United States of America

Table of Contents printed at front instead of at back as in the 1930 edition. Type in Contents for the line "A Further Range" is varied to italics from type used to designate other included books.

Inscription (on title page): To Esther Mertins from Robert Frost At the lovely house in Redlands March 1947.

Second copy. Same, except for words April Printing on verso.

Inscription (on end paper): To Sally Mertins Haverlandt Dewees in friendship. Robert Frost.

I Could Give All to Time

ONLY EDITION [1941]

This Christmas card appeared in three forms: Christmas Greetings from Robert Frost; Christmas Greetings from Henry Holt and Company; and Christmas Greetings from Marguerite and Fred Melcher. Printed on rough white paper, its fold formed the binding. Picture on cover printed in green and brown bears the legend: J. J. Lankes. The card bears no printer's legend or publisher's imprint. The poem appeared in the autumn number of the *Yale Review*, 1941. Later it was included in *A Witness Tree*. Text page bears the following:

I Could Give All to Time / by Robert Frost / [text of poem] / Copyright 1941 by Robert Frost

Inscriptions: (Frost's card) Complete in three vols Vol I Robert Frost to Louis Mertins; (Holt's card) V II Picture of a Witness Tree; (Melcher's card) Vol III.

A Witness Tree

FIRST EDITION, FIRST PRINTING [1942]

This is the first printing of Robert Frost's seventh book; it was soon followed by a second printing. Bound in blue buckram, front cover and spine stamped in gilt. The title page bears the following:

A / Witness / Tree / by / Robert / Frost / Henry Holt and Company / New York

On the verso of the title page appears the legend: First

Printing / Copyright, 1942, by Robert Frost / Printed in the United States of America.

Inscription (on end paper):

> We dance round in a ring and suppose
> But the secret sits in the middle and knows
>
>   ROBERT FROST
> To Louis Mertins
> Cambridge 1943

Second copy, same as the foregoing, except that on the verso of the title page appears the line: Second Printing.

Inscription (on half title): To Louis Mertins from his friend Robert Frost April 1945.

NOTE: This copy bears the complimentary card of the publishers, the book being sent out for the use of reviewers. Louis Mertins used it for reviews in certain newspapers and magazines, including the Los Angeles *Times* and the *Southern Literary Messenger*.

THE GUARDEEN

ONLY EDITION, 1943

This is a Christmas card used by Earle J. Bernheimer in 1943. It is the first draft of the opening act of a proposed play by Robert Frost to be called "The Guardeen." Bound in heavy, rough, buff paper. The greetings appear on front cover in red ink. No end papers. Page one is title page. Page two is a reproduction of Frost's playful "fee simple." Title page contains the following:

The pages, here reproduced from the / original manuscript of the first draft of / an unpublished play by Robert Frost, /

BIBLIOGRAPHY

are printed in an edition of 96 copies by / The Ward Ritchie Press, Los Angeles, / California, for Earle J. Bernheimer. / This is copy number / [nine] / Christmas, 1943. (The number of the copy is written in by Mr. Bernheimer.)

Inscription (on page two): Robert Frost.

COME IN AND OTHER POEMS
FIRST EDITION, FIRST PRINTING [1943]

This is the prepublication copy sent to Louis Mertins by the publishers for reviewing the book in newspapers. No card, however, accompanied it. End papers, colored pictorial of White and Green Mountains. Bound in light tan buckram; printing in reddish brown on front cover and spine. The title page bears the following:

Come In / and Other Poems / by / Robert Frost / Selection, / biographical introduction, / and commentary by / Louis Untermeyer / Illustrated by / John O'Hara Cosgrave II / Henry Holt and Company

On the verso of the title page (under date line, 1943, and source of poems) is the legend: first printing.

Inscription (on half title): To my friend Louis Mertins Robert Frost.

COME IN AND OTHER POEMS
WARTIME EDITION [1944]

This is the "skimpy margin" edition published in wartime. As set forth on the verso of the title page, "This complete edition is produced in compliance with the government's regulations for conserving paper and other essential materials." It has greatly reduced margins and the paper is skimpy, though the same plates have been used as in the first edition. End papers same as those of first edition. Bound in tan cloth, printing, as in first edition, in reddish brown on front cover and spine. The title page bears the following:

Come In / and Other Poems / by / Robert Frost / Selection, / biographical introduction, / and commentary by / Louis Untermeyer / Illustrated by / John O'Hara Cosgrave II / Henry Holt and Company

Inscription (on end paper): Dear Louis: I doubt if this is a first edition, but it at least has the merit of not being of the many from you to me and back again. I mean it is not a mere book of yours I have signed but a gift. Robert. Cambridge Massachusetts October 26 1944.

AN UNSTAMPED LETTER IN OUR RURAL LETTER BOX
ONLY EDITION, FIRST PRINTING [1944]

A complete set of six Christmas cards, in a white envelope on which Robert Frost has written the words "all here." Each card bound in terra-cotta paper; cream stock, printing in brown ink. Not only Frost, Holt, and Thomas W. Nason the artist, but also Ann & Joseph Blumenthal, Marguerite and Fred Melcher, and William Sloane used the Letter as a Christmas card; hence the set. On the front cover the title is printed on a white slip of paper pasted on. The title page bears the following:

An Unstamped Letter / in Our / Rural Letter Box / by / Robert Frost / [drawing by Nason]

BIBLIOGRAPHY

On the half title of the Frost card (uniform for all with change of name) appears: This New Poem / Is Sent to You / with Holiday Goodwill / from / Robert Frost / December 1944.

The first page following text bears the legends: Woodcut by Thomas W. Nason / [star] / Printed at The Spiral Press / [star] / Copyright 1944 by Robert Frost.

Inscription (on half title, interwoven to read): [This new poem] in six imprints [is sent to you] Louis Mertins [with Holiday Goodwill from] your old California friend Robert Frost [December 1944]. The "Robert Frost" is signed as well as printed.

Inscription in second Frost copy (on half title): your laggard friend R.F.

Two Leading Lights
ONLY EDITION, 1944

This is an unpublished poem, used on a Christmas card for Earle J. Bernheimer. Bound in heavy, rough, buff paper. It is an exact companion piece to *The Guardeen,* 1943. The greetings appear on the front cover in red ink. No title page. No end papers. Page one of text shows reproduction of telegram, yellow background on fine white paper, sent to Bernheimer from Kathleen Morrison, December 6, 1944, relative to the poem for a Christmas card. Page three reproduces the MS of the poem. Page four bears the following:

This hitherto unpublished poem by / Robert Frost is limited to 52 copies, / Printed by the Ward Ritchie Press, / Los Angeles, California, for / Earle J. Bernheimer. / This is copy number [nine]. / Christmas, 1944 (The number of the copy is written in by Bernheimer, who inscribed it: Louis Mertins, Cordially, Earle Bernheimer.)

Inscription (on page three): Robert Frost to Louis Mertins.

A Masque of Reason
First edition, first printing [1945]

This is the first printing of the book, the publication of which was synchronized with the poet's seventieth birthday. It is bound in dark blue cloth, front and back blank, gilt lettering vertically along the spine. The title page bears the following:

A Masque / of Reason / by / Robert Frost / Henry Holt and Company / New York

The verso of the title page bears the following: Copyright 1945 by Robert Frost / First Printing / Printed in the United States of America.

Inscription (on half title): Robert Frost to Louis Mertins.

A Young Birch
Only edition [1946]

This poem, printed here for the first time, formed the Christmas card used by Frost and others in 1946. Bound in soft white paper, with decorations in gray and tan. The cover folds front-and-back over end papers, forming a flap. The title page bears the following:

A Young Birch / [decoration] / Robert Frost

The half title bears greetings and date of 1946.

The verso of the half title bears the legend: Copyright / 1946 / by Robert Frost.

Page six bears the legend: Decorations by Joseph Low / [decoration] / Printed at the Spiral Press.

Inscription (on half title of the Frost card): Foretaste and promise of whole set of imprints for L.M. from R.F.

Second copy, included in the whole set mentioned in inscription above. Others who used the card, besides Frost and Holt, were Ann and Joseph Blumenthal, Siri Andrews, Denver Lindley, Joseph A. Brandt, Marguerite and Fred Melcher, Alfred C. Edwards, Joe Duffy, and Ruth and Joseph Low.

Inscription (on Frost's card): To Louis Mertins from R F.

THE POCKET BOOK OF ROBERT FROST'S POEMS

FIRST PRINTING, APRIL [1946]

This is the first edition of Robert Frost's poems to be offered at a reduced price, unless we except the Halcyon House edition of the *Collected Poems*. It was published in the twenty-five cent series by Pocket Books, Inc., and carried the same selection of poems as were printed in *Come In,* the publishers stating that an additional thirty poems were included. The biographical commentary by Louis Untermeyer was only slightly enlarged. The pictures by Cosgrave, however, were improved and softened in tone by being printed in green ink. The book was printed from new plates. Bound in heavy paper. Color plate, frontispiece for *Come In,* on the cover. End papers bright red, inside cover page same. The title page reads as follows.

The Pocket Book of / Robert Frost's / Poems / [picture of woods and wall] / with an Introduction and Commentary by / Louis Untermeyer / [colophon] / Pocket Books, Inc. New York

Inscription (on end paper): To Louis from Robert 1947.

Second copy, same except for words September Printing on verso.

Inscription (on end paper): U.S.A. 1946 King's X
>Having invented a new Holocaust
>And been the first with it to win a war
>How they make haste to cry with fingers crossed
>"King's X, no fairs to use it any more."

To Louis Mertins. Calif 1947   Robert Frost

The Poems of Robert Frost
First Modern Library Edition [1946]

Random House issued this slightly abbreviated edition of *The Collected Poems of Robert Frost* late in 1946. It contains all the poems in his first six books found in the Halcyon House edition, together with those contained in *A Witness Tree*, with this exception: thirty-six poems have been omitted. "The Pasture," which appeared in the first edition of *North of Boston* on page vii, and was not there included in the table of contents, and which in the first and second editions of *The Collected Poems* occupies about the same position, being also left out of the table of contents, here takes its place incorrectly as part of *A Boy's Will*, and is listed in the table of contents. One poem (the unorthodox sonnet which accompanies the Introductory Essay), not in any

BIBLIOGRAPHY 83

previous book, is added. This poem, "To the Right Person," appeared with the essay, "The Constant Symbol," in the *Atlantic Monthly* for October, 1946. The book is bound in green buckram, gold lettering on black background front cover and spine. End papers gray and white. The title page bears the following:

The Poems / of / Robert / Frost / with an Introductory Essay / "The Constant Symbol" / by the Author / [colophon] / [line] / The Modern Library . New York / [line]

On the verso of the title page appear the various copyright legends and publisher's advertisement. Copyright, 1930, 1939, by Henry Holt & Co., Inc. / Copyright, 1936, 1942, by Robert Frost / Copyright, 1946, by Random House, Inc. / First Modern Library Edition, 1946 / [decoration] / Random House is the Publisher of / The Modern Library / Bennett A. Cerf . Donald S. Klopfer . Robert K. Haas / Manufactured in the United States of America / Printed by Parkway Printing Company. Bound by H. Wolff.

Inscription (on title page): To Louis from Robert 1947.

STEEPLE BUSH
FIRST EDITION [1947]

This, Robert Frost's eighth book of poems, was published by Henry Holt and Company in May, 1947. Bound in light green cloth; title and author's name lengthwise of spine and reading downward, in gold on black, with a gold border; publisher's name, Holt, across foot of spine, in black. The book contains forty-three poems, many of which had appeared in magazines in recent months. Some had been used as Christmas cards, including "A Young Birch," "An Unstamped Letter in Our Rural Letter Box," and "Two Leading Lights." The title page bears the following:

Steeple Bush / by / Robert Frost / [colophon] / New York / Henry Holt and Company

On the verso of the title page appears the legend: Copyright 1947 by Henry Holt and Company · Inc / Printed in the United States of America.

The book has two half titles, one of which is page 1.

Index

Abercrombie, Lascelles, 24, 25
"Acquainted with the Night," 50
"Across the Atlantic," 22, 40
Acton, Massachusetts, 43
Adams, John Walcott, drawings in *Century Magazine*, 21
"After Apple-Picking," 21
"After-Flakes," 9, 52
American Literature, 55
American Mercury, 35, 51, 52, 54
Amherst, 1, 29–34, 35, 43–54, 73
Amherst Monthly, 50
Anthony, Joseph, 33, 45
"Armful, The," 37, 50
Articles about Frost in: *Current Opinion*, 42; *Independent*, 43; *New Republic*, 44; *Bookman*, 48–49; *Current Reviews*, 49; *Scholastic*, 50; *Virginia Quarterly Review*, 51; *Saturday Review of Literature*, 54; *The Month at Goodspeed's*, 57; *New Hampshire Troubadour*, 58; *Daily Californian*, 59
"Astrometaphysical," 36, 58
"At Woodward's Gardens," 12, 53
Atlantic Monthly, 9, 22, 25, 28, 33, 35, 36–37, 42, 43, 44, 47–48, 54, 55, 56, 58, 59, 83
"Atmosphere" ("Inscription for a Garden Wall"), 50
"Axe-Helve, The," 33, 44
Augustan Books of Poetry, *Robert Frost*, 68

Baptiste, 21
Beaconsfield, 26
"Bear, The," 50
"Bearer of Evil Tidings, The," 9, 53
Benét, William Rose, article about Frost, 54
"Bereft," 11, 49
Bernheimer, Earle J., 76–77, 79–80
Best Poems of 1923, poem in, 47
Birch tree, 2
"Birches," 19, 28, 42
"Blood" ("The Flood"), 50
"Blue-Butterfly Day," 45
"Blue Ribbon at Amesbury, A," 19, 22, 53
"Blueberries," 21, 54
"Bonfire, The," 23, 33, 43, 44
Bookman: review of *North of Boston*, 41; poem in, 47; article by Dorothy Canfield Fisher, 48–49
Books: *Robert Frost: A Chronological Survey*, 54; *Recognition of Robert Frost*, 55; *Robert Frost and the Sound of Sense*, 55; *Some Notes on Robert Frost and Shakespere*, 55; *Robert Frost: A Bibliography*, 55; *A Chat with Robert Frost*, 56; *Fifty Years of Robert Frost*, 58
Borzoi Chap Books, 15, 69
"Boundless Moment, A," 47
Boy's Will, A: Derry poems, 10, 20, 40, 51, 82; "My Butterfly," 13, 37, 39; published, 27; reviewed by

Boy's Will, A—Continued
  Ezra Pound, 28, and by William Dean Howells, 42–43; first editions, 61, 64, 65
"Bravery," 36, 59
"Brook in the City, A," 45
Brooke, Rupert, 24, 25, 33
Browne, George H., article about Frost, 43
"Build Soil," 15
Bust of Frost, 63
"But He Meant It," 37, 59

"Caesar's Transport Ships," 14, 15
California, 1, 2, 3, 5, 7, 8 ff., 33, 52, 64. *See also* San Francisco
Cambridge, 34–35, 78
"Carpe Diem," 55
"Census Taker, The," 45
Century Magazine, 21, 43, 46
Charles Eliot Norton professorship of poetry, 34
Chat with Robert Frost, A, by Cyril Clemens, 56
Christmas cards: "Neither Out Far nor In Deep," 6, 71; "Two Tramps in Mud-time," 70; "To a Young Wretch," 73; "I Could Give All to Time," 75; "The Guardeen," 76–77; "An Unstamped Letter in Our Rural Mail Box," 78–79, 84; "Two Leading Lights," 79–80, 84; "A Young Birch," 80–81, 84
Citizen, 8, 52
Clark, Sylvia, 55
Cleghorn, Sarah, 48–49
Clemens, Cyril, *A Chat with Robert Frost*, 56
Cliff House, 8, 9, 54
Clymer, W. B. Shubrick, *Robert Frost: A Bibliography*, 55

"Cocoon, The," 49
"Code, The," 21, 41
Collected Poems, 1, 13, 37, 48, 56, 68, 73–74, 81, 82
Colum, Padraic, review of *Mountain Interval*, 44
"Come In," 56
Come In and Other Poems, 37, 77–78, 81, 82
"Common Fate, The," 50
"Considerable Speck, A," 56
"Constant Symbol, The" (prose), 58, 83
Contemporary American Men Poets, 7, 54
Cosgrave, John O'Hara, II, 77, 78, 81
"Cow in Apple Time, The," 28, 41
"Cow's in the Corn, The," 50
Craftsman, 43
Cranston, Earl, 38
Current Opinion: article about Frost, 42; poems, 47
Current Reviews, essay by Gorman B. Munson, 49

Daily Californian, article by Ruth Ray, 59
Dartmouth, 34; Baker Library exhibition, 36
Dartmouth in Portrait, poems, 58
Dearborn Independent, 48, 50
"Departmental," 53
Derry, New Hampshire, 2, 10, 13, 16, 18–24, 29, 35, 39–40, 43, 53, 57
Derry News, 22
"Desert Places," 35, 51
De Vries, Virginia Mertins, 69
Dewees, Sally Mertins Haberlandt, 74
"Directive," 36, 58

INDEX

Doughty, John, 12–13; *The Parable*, 59
Dreiser, Theodore, 51
Drinkwater, John, 24
"Drumlin Woodchuck, A," 54
Du Chêne, Aroldo, bust by, 63
Dudley, Dorothy, 51
"Dust of Snow" ("Snow Dust"), 45
Dymock, Gloucestershire, 10, 11, 24–29, 40–43

"Encounter, An," 43
England, 24–29 *passim*, 48
"Etherealizing," 37, 59

"Fear, The," 28, 41
Fifty Years of Robert Frost, edited by Ray Nash, 58
"Figure in the Doorway, The," 53
"Fire and Ice," 45
Fisher, Dorothy Canfield, article about Frost, 48–49
Flint, F. S., 26; letter to Pound, 27
"Flood, The" ("Blood"), 50
"Flower Boat, The," 15, 23, 40
"Flower-Gathering," 20
"For Once, Then, Something," 45
Forgotten Frontiers, letter to Mencken in, 51
Forum, 19, 24, 40
"Fountain, a Bottle, a Donkey's Ears and Some Books, A," 47
"Fragmentary Blue," 45
Franconia farm, 20, 21, 43
Frost, Elinor White, 20, 21, 48, 70, 71
Frost family, 10, 15, 19, 34
Further Range, A, 12, 35, 38, 51–54, 60, 69, 70, 72–74

"Gathering Leaves," 47
"Ghost House," 15

Gibson, Wilfrid, 24; "The Golden Room," 25, 47–48; review of *North of Boston*, 41
"Gift Outright, The," 57
"Going for Water," 20
Gold Hesperidee, The, 70–71
Golden Book Magazine, 51
"Golden Room, The," Gibson's poem about Frost, 25, 47–48
"Good-Bye and Keep Cold," 45
"Good Hours," 74
Green, Charles R., *Robert Frost: A Bibliography*, 55
Greystone house (Monrovia), 8
"Guardeen, The" (play), 76–77, 79
"Gum-Gatherer, The," 43

"Haec Fabula Docet," 36, 59
"Hannibal," 15
Hanover, 34, 36–38, 57–59
"Happiness Makes Up in Height for What It Lacks in Length," 55
Harper's Magazine, 33, 42–43, 45
"Hill Wife, The," 42
"Hillside Thaw, A," 33, 38, 45
"Home Burial," 21
Howells, William Dean, review of *North of Boston* and *A Boy's Will*, 42–43
"Hundred Collars, A," 28, 41

"I Could Give All to Time," 56, 75
"I Will Sing You One-O," 37, 47
"Importer, The," 37, 59
"In a Disused Graveyard," 15, 38
"In Hardwood Groves" ("The Same Leaves"), 48
"In the Home Stretch," 21, 38, 43
"In the Long Night," 57–58
"In Time of Cloudburst," 53
Independent, 3, 10, 13, 14, 22, 39, 40, 42, 43

"Ingenuities of Debt, The," 36, 59
"Inscription for a Garden Wall" ("Atmosphere"), 50
"Into Mine Own" ("Into My Own"), 6, 19, 23, 40
"Iris by Night," 26, 53

Key West, 30-31

Ladies' Home Journal, 50-51
Land's End, 5, 11
Lankes, J. J., 49, 54, 57, 65, 66, 67, 71, 73, 75
"Late Walk, A," 20, 38
Lawrence, Massachusetts, 1, 6, 13-18, 20, 29, 39, 45
Lawrence High School *Bulletin*, 6, 14
"Leaf-Treader, A," 52
"Lesson for To-day, The," 30-31
"Line-storm Song, A," 19, 22, 40
"Literate Farmer and the Planet Venus, The," 9, 12, 56
"Little Iddens" farm, 24, 25
"Lodged," 47
Lone Striker, A, 15, 51, 69
Long Beach, 9, 54
Long Island, 9
Los Angeles *Times*, 76
"Lost Faith, The," 22
"Love and a Question," 15
Lowe, Orton, article about Frost, 50
Lowell, Amy, review of *North of Boston*, 42

Maine coast, 12
"Maple," 38, 46
Marginalia, 59
Martin, Keith, portrait by, 58
Masque of Reason, A (play), 80
"Master Speed," 53
Meiklejohn, Alexander, 29, 46

Mencken, H. L., 51
"Mending Wall," 18, 21, 47
Merrimack River, 14
Mertins, Esther, inscription to, 74
Mertins, Louis: first acquaintance with Frost, 1; collection, 1-3; inscriptions to, 7, 8, 9, 14, 16, 19, 22, 27, 30, 33, 39-59 *passim*, 61-83 *passim*; "A Sheaf of Verse," 52; review of *A Witness Tree*, in the *Southern Literary Messenger*, 57
"Middleness of the Road, The," 36, 58
"Minor Bird, The," 50
"Misgiving," 45
"Missive Missile, A," 52
Modern Library, *The Poems of Robert Frost*, 13, 37, 38, 58, 82-83
Monroe, Harriet, review of *Mountain Interval*, 44
Monrovia, California, 1
Month at Goodspeed's, The, article about Frost, 57
"Moon Compasses," 52
Morrison, Kathleen, 13, 39, 55, 79
"Moth Found in Winter, A," 16
Mountain Interval: of Plymouth days, 10-11; published, 31; reviewed by Padraic Colum, 44, and by Harriet Monroe, 44; poems in, 42, 43, 44; first edition, 64-65
"Mowing," 20
Munro, Harold, 26, 27, 28
Munson, Gorman B., essay on Frost, 49
"My Butterfly: An Elegy," 3, 13, 14, 37, 39, 43
"My November Guest," 6, 19, 24, 40

"Name Unnamed" ("Untried," "Waspish"), 30, 53

INDEX

Nash, Ray, edited *Fifty Years of Robert Frost*, 36, 58
Nason, Thomas W., 79
Nation, 45, 50
"Need of Being Versed in Country Things, The," 45, 50
"Neither Out Far nor In Deep," 6, 7, 16, 51, 52, 54, 69, 71
New England Magazine, 22, 23, 40
New Frontier, 35, 52
New Hampshire, 10, 11, 19, 21
New Hampshire, 11; published, 31, 32; poems in, 44-47 *passim*, 50; first edition, 65, 66
New Hampshire Troubadour, Robert Frost Issue, 36, 58-59
New Jerusalem, Society of the, 12
New Republic: poems in, 8, 33, 45-49 *passim;* review of *North of Boston*, 42; review of *Mountain Interval*, 44; article by Lola Ridge, 44
Newdick, Robert S.: *Robert Frost and the Sound of Sense*, 55; *Some Notes on Robert Frost and Shakespere*, 55
"Night Light, The," 36, 59
"No Holy Wars for Them," 37, 59
"Nocturnes," 36, 59
North of Boston: New Hampshire product, 10, 21; published, 27; reviewed by: Wilfrid Gibson, 41, Ezra Pound, 41, Amy Lowell, 42, William Dean Howells, 42-43; first edition, 62, 82; second American edition, 63; advertised, 65
"Not Quite Social," 52
"Not to Keep," 33, 44
"Nothing Gold Can Stay," 6, 34, 47, 54, 66
"November," 34
"Now Close the Window," 21

"October," 24
"Of the Stones of the Place" ("Rich in Stones"), 34-35, 57
Old Farmer's Almanac, 34, 54, 57
"Old Man's Winter Night, An," 66
Old Nailshop ("the Golden Room"), 25, 38
"On a Bird Singing in Its Sleep," 52
"On the Heart's Beginning to Cloud the Mind," 30, 35, 51
"Once by the Pacific," 8, 11, 49
"Once Down on My Knees," 36, 58
"Onset, The," 45
"Our Getaway," 36, 58-59
"Our Singing Strength," 46
"Oven Bird, The," 66

"Pan With Us," 15, 38
Parable of Creation, The, by John Doughty, 59
"Passing Glimpse, The," 48
"Pasture, The," 19, 82
"Paul's Wife," 33, 46
"Pauper Witch of Grafton, The," 37, 45
"Peck of Gold, A," 11
Photographs and silhouettes, 60
Pinkerton Academy, 18, 55
"Place for a Third," 45
"Planners, The," 37, 59
Plymouth, 11, 24
Pocket Books, 37, 81-82
Poems of Today, poem in, 47
Poetry: A Magazine of Verse, 28, 30, 35, 41, 44, 53
Poetry and Drama, 27, 28, 41-42
Poetry Bookshop, Bloomsbury, 27, 41
Portraits, 58, 74
Pound, Ezra, 26, 27-28; reviewed *A Boy's Will*, 28, 41, and *North of Boston*, 41

"Prayer in Spring, A," 20
"Provide Provide," 52
Pulitzer Prize, 35
"Putting in the Seed," 28, 41

"Quest of the Orchis, The" ("The Quest of the Purple-Fringed"), 16–18, 22, 39

Ray, Ruth, article about Frost, 59
Recognition of Robert Frost, 55
"Record Stride, A," 9, 54
"Reluctance," 51
Reviews: *A Boy's Will*, 28, 41, 42–43; *North of Boston*, 41, 42–43; *Mountain Interval*, 44; *Collected Poems*, 56; *A Witness Tree*, 57
"Rich in Stones" ("Of the Stones of the Place"), 34–35, 57
Ridge, Lola, article about Frost, 44
Ripton, Vermont, 2, 20, 24, 35, 43, 47
"Road Not Taken, The," 26, 28, 42
"Roadside Stand, A," 54
Robert Frost: A Bibliography, by W. B. Shubrick Clymer and Charles R. Green, 55
Robert Frost: A Chronological Survey, 54
Robert Frost and the Sound of Sense, by Robert S. Newdick, 55
"Rogers Group, A," 36, 59
"Rose Family, The," 50
"Rose Pogonias," 20
Rueb, Emile, portrait by, 58
"Runaway, The," 50, 66
Ryton firs, 10

"Same Leaves, The" ("In Hardwood Groves"), 48
San Francisco, 5–13
"Sand Dunes," 12, 48

Saturday Review of Literature: poems in, 10, 52, 70; article about Frost, 54; portrait, 58
Scholastic, article about Frost, 50
Scribner's Magazine, 30, 35, 51, 52
Selected Poems, 69–70
"Serious Step Lightly Taken, A," 31
Seven Arts, The, 24, 43
Several Short Poems, 66
Shakespeare Association *Bulletin*, 55
"Silken Tent, The," 56
"Smile, The," 28, 41, 42
"Snow," 44
"Snow Dust" ("Dust of Snow"), 45
Some Notes on Robert Frost and Shakespere, by Robert S. Newdick, 55
"Something for Hope," 36, 59
"Sound of Trees, The," 10, 28, 41, 42
South Shaftsbury, Vermont, 9, 20, 33, 53, 54
Southern Literary Messenger, review of *A Witness Tree*, 57; card, 76
"Spring Pools," 50
"Star in a Stone-Boat, A," 45
"Star-Splitter, The," 46–47
"Stars," 15
Steeple Bush, 38, 83–84
"Stopping by Woods on a Snowy Evening," 1, 33, 46, 47, 66
"Storm Fear," 20–21
"Strong Are Saying Nothing, The," 54
"Subverted Flower, The," 37

"Telephone, The," 43
"Ten Mills," 30, 35, 53
"Thatch, The," 26, 38
"They Were Welcome to Their Belief," 52

Thomas, Edward, 24, 25, 26, 33
Three Poems, poem in, 16, 39
Time: review of *Collected Poems*, 56; review of *A Witness Tree*, 57
"Time Out," 57
"Times Table, The," 49
"To a Moth Seen in Winter," 57
"To a Young Wretch," 73
"To an Ancient," 37, 59
"To E. T.," 11, 25–26, 44
"To Earthward," 47
"To the Right Person," 83
"To the Thawing Wind," 21
Torrence, Ridgely, 48
Treasury of War Poetry, A, poem in, 44
"Tree at My Window," 2, 22, 50
"Trespass," 22
"Trial by Existence," 10, 22, 37, 40
"Trial Run, A," 54
"Tuft of Flowers, A," 18, 19, 20
Twilight, 13
"Two Leading Lights," 79–80, 84
"Two Tramps in Mud-time," 70

Ulmann, Doris, portrait by, 74
"Unstamped Letter in Our Rural Letter Box, An," 78–79, 84
Untermeyer, Louis, 28, 37, 77, 78, 81, 82
"U.S. 1946 King's X," 36–37, 59, 82

"Valley's Singing Day, The," 45
"Vanishing Red, The," 43
Vermont, 2, 9, 19, 22
Virginia Quarterly Review, 26, 36, 50, 53, 56, 57, 58; article about Frost, 51
"Voice-Ways," 53

Wall, 2, 21
"Warning," 14
Way Out, A (play), 29, 67
"Were I in Trouble with Night Tonight," 36, 59
West Midlands, Gloucestershire, 10, 24, 26
West-running Brook: California echoes in, 11, 12; West-running Brook landscape, 18; published, 31, 32; reviewers' neglect of, 32; poems in, 40, 47–51 *passim*; first edition, 66–67
White, Elinor. *See* Frost, Elinor White
White Mountains, 12, 18
"White-tailed Hornet or Doubts about an Instinct, The," 53
"Wild Grapes," 45
Wilkesbarre, Pennsylvania, 30, 51
Wilson, James Southall, article by, 51
"Wind and Window Flower," 20–21, 38
"Winter Eden, A," 33, 49
"Witch of Coos, The," 33, 46
Witness Tree, A: poems in, 12, 16, 22, 30, 34, 35, 37, 55, 56, 57, 73, 75, 82; reviewed in *Time*, 57; reviewed by Louis Mertins, 57; first edition, 75–76
"Woodpile, The," 21, 27
Woodward's Gardens, 5, 12

Yale Review, 6, 7, 8, 9, 25, 33, 35, 36, 44, 45, 46, 47, 50, 51, 52, 53, 56, 59, 71, 75
"Young Birch, A," 80–81, 84
Youth's Companion, 23, 24, 40, 51

www.ingramcontent.com/pod-product-compliance
Lightning Source LLC
Chambersburg PA
CBHW021716230426
43668CB00008B/847